INFORMATION MODELLING
- FOR BUSINESS AND BEYOND

Cura Viewpoint No.2

Bob Wiggins

Copyright © 2019 Bob Wiggins

First edition March 2016 in e-book
Updated edition April 2019
All rights reserved

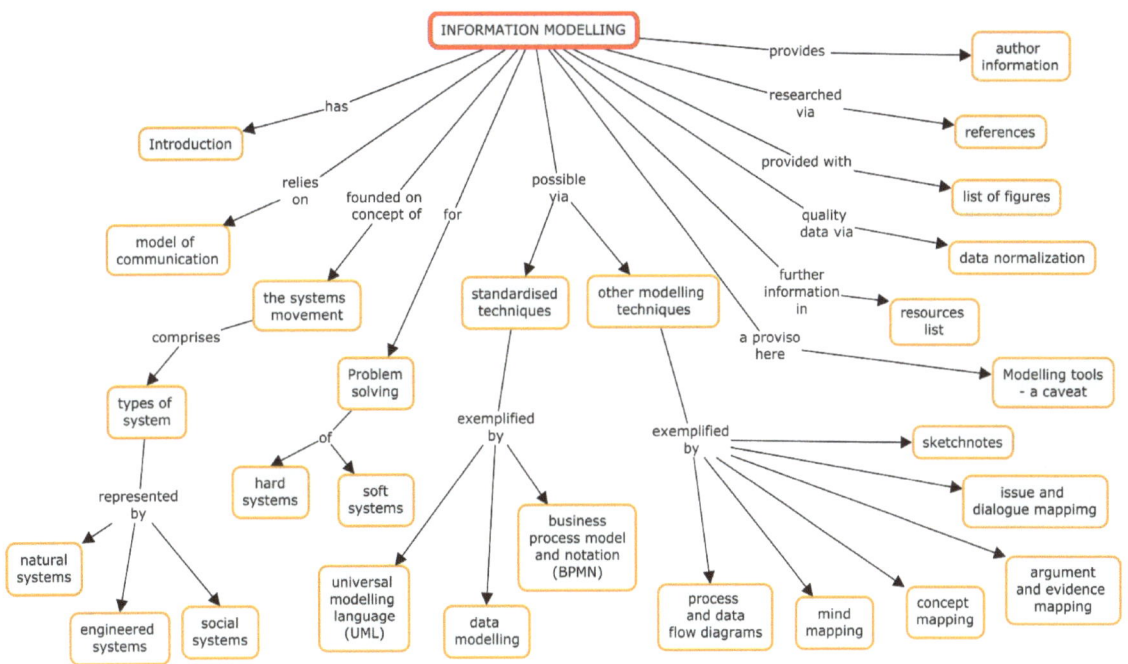

Concept map of the Viewpoint's content (Created using Cmap Tools)

Table of Contents

INTRODUCTION 5
   Note for paperback edition 5
A MODEL OF COMMUNICATION 6
THE SYSTEMS MOVEMENT 7
   Development of the Systems Movement 7
   Criticisms of the System Approach 7
   Scope of this Viewpoint 9
TYPES OF SYSTEMS 10
   A natural system - Modelling electron waves 11
   An engineered system - Modelling beam bridge construction 11
   A social system - Modelling Galapagos social-ecological system 13
PROBLEM SOLVING METHODOLOGIES 15
   Hard System Methodologies 15
   Soft System Methodologies 18
   Comparison of hard and soft methodologies 21
STANDARDISED MODELLING METHODS 23
   Universal Modelling Language (UML) 23
   Data Modelling 29
   Business Process Model and Notation (BPMN) 34
   The relationship between data analysis and process analysis 38
OTHER MODELLING TECHNIQUES 39
PROCESS AND DATA FLOW DIAGRAMS 41
   Data Flow Diagrams 41
   Flow charts 42
MIND MAPPING 44
CONCEPT MAPPING 46
ARGUMENT AND EVIDENCE MAPPING 48
   Evidence Gap Mapping 50
ISSUE AND DIALOGUE MAPPING 51
   Issue Mapping 51
   Dialogue mapping 54
SKETCHNOTES 54
MODELLING TOOLS – A CAVEAT 56
RESOURCES LIST 57

ANNEX A DATA NORMALIZATION 60
LIST OF FIGURES 63
REFERENCES 65
AUTHOR INFORMATION 70

INTRODUCTION

This second in a series of Cura Viewpoints is concerned with the use of modelling techniques to address matter of concern, whether encountered in business or beyond as an individual. Models (and what may also be more generally called diagrams, drawings or pictures) are often used to help deal with complexity, promote understanding or preserve and reuse knowledge.

Any matter that one might decide to model will be bounded in some way by physical or mental constructs, i.e. it constitutes the system under consideration. There is also the need to communicate about the matter. The Viewpoint therefore commences by considering a model for communication and then addresses the systems movement itself. Types of systems - social, natural and engineered - are then explained and exemplified to provide a foundation for discussion of the different types of methodologies and methods for tackling 'hard' and 'soft' problems.

The Viewpoint then addresses the modelling techniques that have some formalised or standardised approach, such as the Universal Modelling Language (UML), and the modelling of data and processes and their inter-relationship. The remainder of the Viewpoint covers the extensive range of generalised or specialised techniques that have emerged such as mind and concept mapping which have wide applicability, to issue and evidence mapping which are more focussed in their intent.

A resources list provides additional sources of information to the various references cited as bracketed numbers.

Note for the updated edition

The references and resources have been reviewed and updated where necessary. However, hyperlinks were used at the times indicated and their validity after that date cannot be guaranteed.

A MODEL OF COMMUNICATION

The ability to communicate information effectively and efficiently is a vital component of the problem-solving process. So in the context of this Viewpoint it is informative to examine the elements of communication by way of a model.

Communication is defined as *'the transmission or exchange of information, news, etc'*. (1).

The process of communication was first modelled by Shannon and Weaver in 1949 (2) as shown in (Figure 1). It mirrors the functions of radio and telegraph technologies. The information source produces the message which is encoded into signals by the transmitter. The encoded message is sent through an appropriate channel to the receiver which decodes the signals to produce the message for the destination. The channel of communication may be face-to-face or through intermediary technology such as email and social media. The message typically involves the written word, speech and visual media, although gestures and sensory information such as touch or smell might form part.

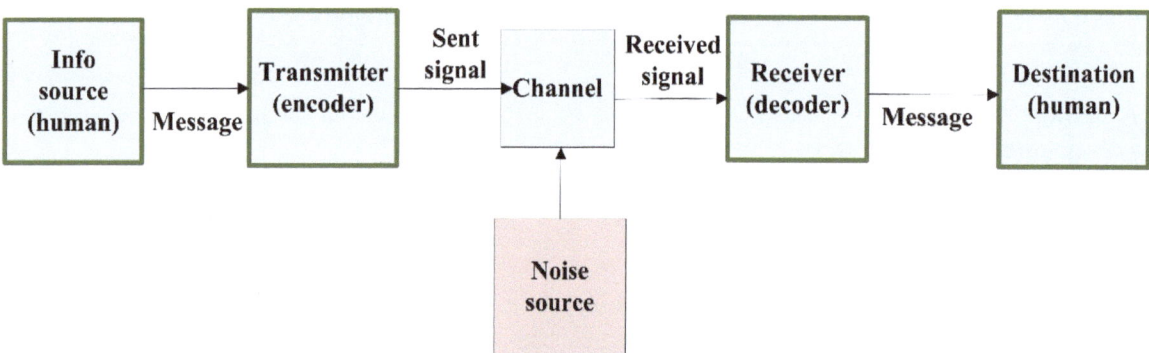

Figure 1 Shannon and Wear Communication Model (Created using MS Visio 2007)

As regards the noise source, Adler and Towne (3) suggested that the interference in communication might be physical, such as noisy and distracting backgrounds or psychological where the mental state of the recipient impairs understanding. Further problems can arise where words have different meanings for the source and destination; they may also speak different languages and the encoding is unable to deal with language translation.

Since its inception the model has been the subject of much debate and development in the academic world, often to produce revised models termed, for example, constructionist, linear, interactive and transactional (4).

Although the model has been criticised for over-simplifying human communication (for example it takes no account of any two-way communication relating to the message) it does provide a way to focus on the key components in a communication chain and any associated problems.

THE SYSTEMS MOVEMENT

Problems will vary depending on their degree of complexity. Complexity relates to matters that are *'intricate, not easily analysed or disentangled, complicated'* (1). Complexity is an area of concern in many spheres where systems grow or develop beyond a simple, readily comprehended and manageable state. For example, successful start-up organisations have to deal with the problems of growth or take-over, countries must manage their economies in a competing world and the world itself is affected by often unpredictable climate changes.

A range of approaches have emerged to address these types of mega-problem; often reliant on modelling to break the whole down to manageable proportions. Many of the approaches rest within an area of study relating to systems, whose origins can be traced back to the Austrian-born biologist Karl Ludwig von Bertalanffy (5) and his General System Theory (GST) first expounded in 1945.

He defined a system as *'a set of elements in interaction'*. Subsequently *'system'* has been defined by the International Standards Organisation (6) as *'a combination of interacting elements organized to achieve one or more stated purposes'*. In this context a system element can be anything from physical objects to humans or intangible software to processes.

Development of the Systems Movement

Systems theory and practice has evolved over the years to embrace a wide range of disciplines. More recently the term 'systems praxis' has been used to describe the entire intellectual and practical endeavour of creating holistic solutions to complex system challenges (7). This arose from a joint project of the International Council on Systems Engineering (INCOSE) and the International Society for the Systems Sciences (ISSS) to create a Systems Praxis Framework (Figure 2) designed to give systems researchers and practitioners a way to recognize and appreciate the complementary roles played by all participants and stakeholders in the complex process of systems praxis.

Criticisms of the System Approach

Systems theory is broad in its scope and can be termed a meta-discipline as it concerned with integrating a multitude of different sciences, disciplines and areas of study to understand, analyse and influence the various bounded territories in which humans reside or with which they interface or coexist. Although those working in these different areas may use the same terminology they are often divided by a common language as they ascribe different meanings or interpretations to them. This is evidenced by the frequent provision in the SEBoK glossary (8) of competing definitions for the same term. Much time is spent and many academic publications are penned circumscribing the definitions the authors wish to pin down. These differences often lead to obfuscation in discussions, even between those supposedly of like mind.

The General Systems Theory, which effectively formed the starting point for the system movement, has itself been argued against over the years. Thus Thayer (9), an opponent of GST believed that it has failed to deliver because of its own basic assumptions. The concept of hierarchy in GST forces us to impersonalize all social interaction, thus making it impossible to realize ourselves. He felt that GST remained tied to 'laws' of growth which promised only our destruction.

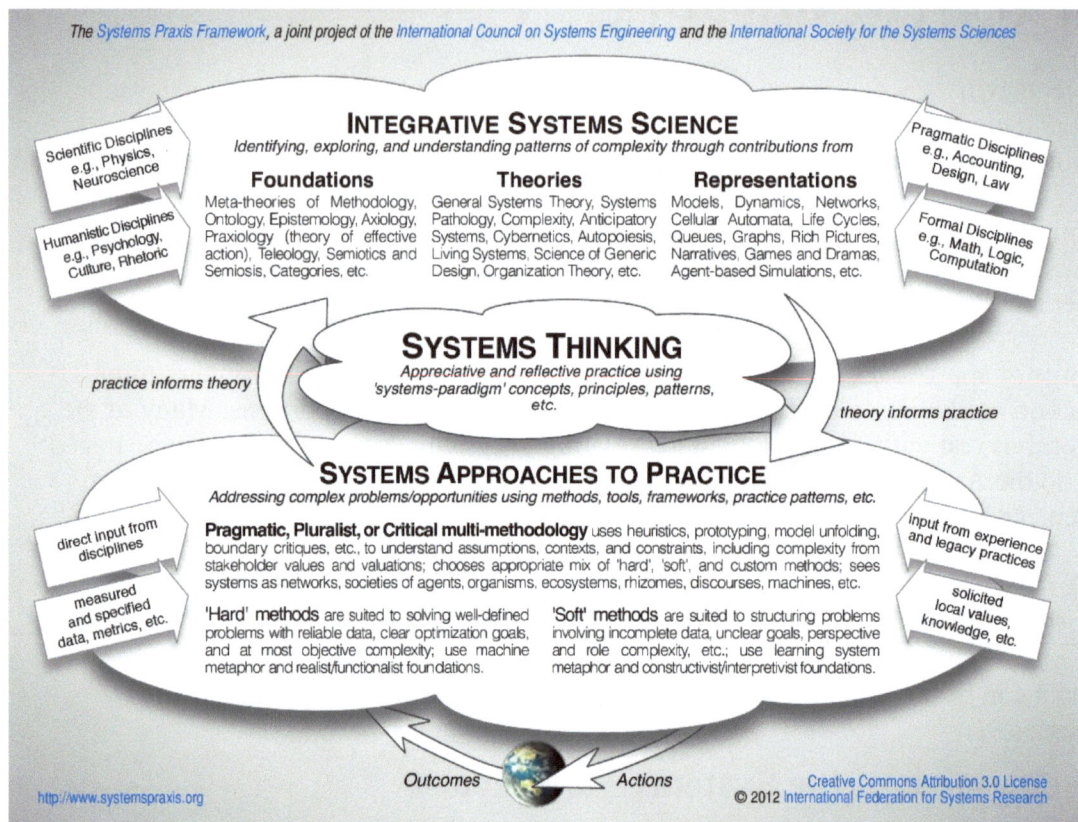

Figure 2 The Systems Praxis Framework (7)

Hale (10), in her focus on organizational communication, highlights other criticisms of GST which, in trying to apply the systems concepts of consensus, growth and hierarchy to organizational administration, fails to take note of intra-organizational conflict, diversity of values and role of the individual.

A major plank of systems theory is to analogize the situation through models and metaphors. The GST seeks to find both similarities and differences between systems, although the tendency is to concentrate on the former without testing any assumptions. Systems analysis arose from its background in solving military and engineering problems and to apply this approach to the public sphere is not tenable, according to Hoos (11).

Leighninger (12) in his article on systems theory and its application to society contends that the macro-level focus of systems theory is unlikely to provide justifiable guidance to practice, but within its broad scope does offer a variety of micro-practical theories and techniques.

He, like others, raised the challenge of deciding the boundaries of a system; what is part of the system and what lies outside in the environment. As Cox and Forshaw (13) noted, no system of objects is perfectly isolated. They took the example of a microwave oven whose operation one might reasonably assume is unaffected by any traffic passing or by stray magnetic fields. Nevertheless, one might erroneously ignore something because some crucial detail is missed. If this happens, the findings will be false and original assumptions will have to be reconsidered.

Scope of this Viewpoint

In this Viewpoint the emphasis is primarily on real world applications and problem solving, and more particularly the role played by 'representations' (models, maps etc) as depicted in Figure 3. For those wishing to delve further into subject of systems theory and systems thinking please consult the References and Resources List.

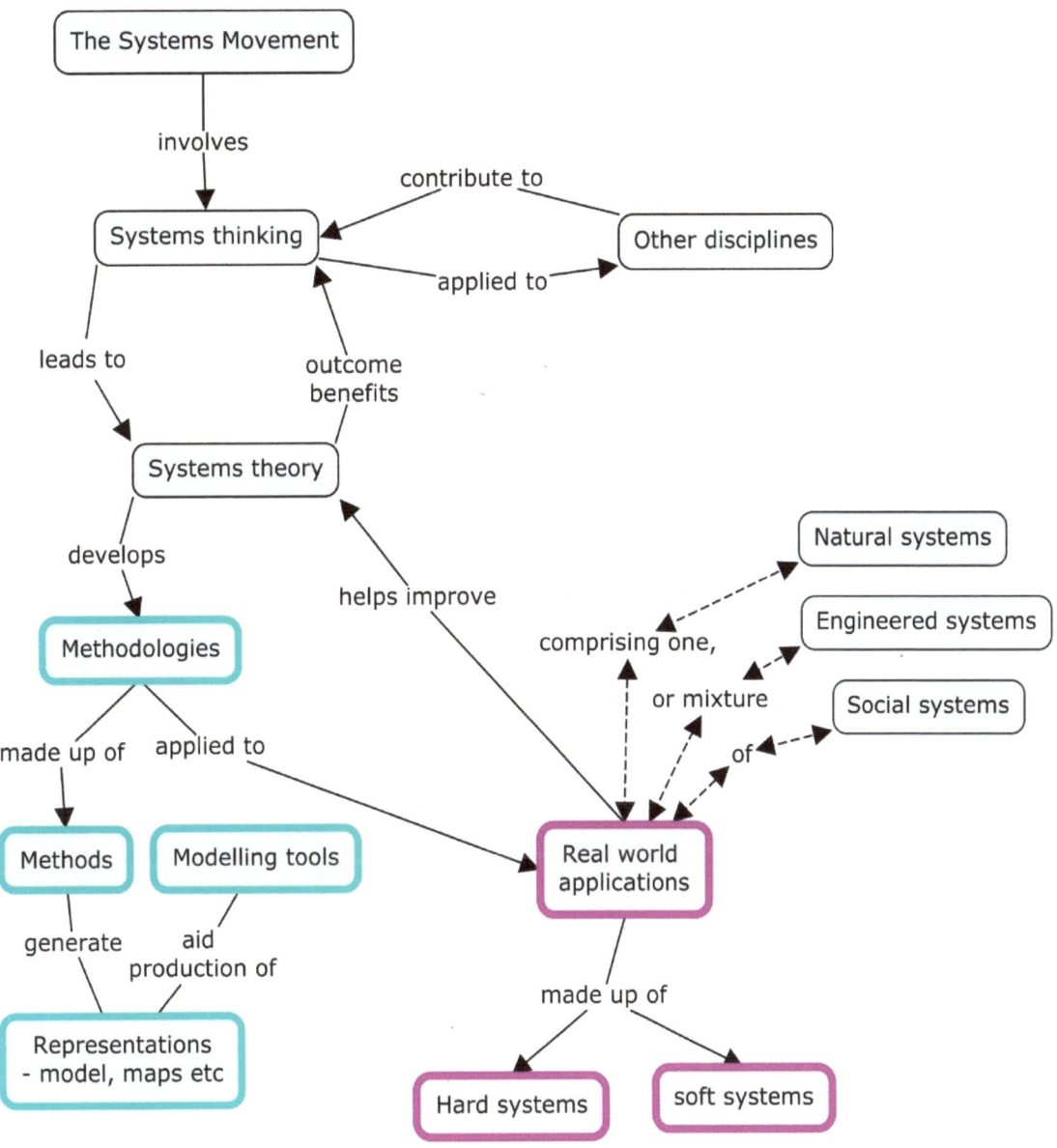

Figure 3 The Systems Movement
(Created using Cmap Tools (http://cmap.ihmc.us/products/))

TYPES OF SYSTEMS

The System Engineering Book of Knowledge (SEBoK) (7) identifies three interlinking systems - Social, Natural and Engineered as represented in (Figure 4). These are defined in their glossary (8) as:

Natural system: *'an open system whose elements, boundary and relationships exist independently of human control'*,

Engineered system: *'an open, concrete system of technical or sociotechnical elements that exhibit emergent properties not exhibited by the individual elements. Its characteristics include being created by and for people; having a purpose, with multiple views; satisfying key stakeholders' value propositions; having a life cycle and evolution dynamics; having a boundary and an external environment; and being a part of a system-of-interest hierarchy'*

and finally

Social system: *'an open system which includes human elements'*.

Examples of the types of system that arise due to these overlaps is shown in the figure and include flood control systems (at the overlap between natural and engineered systems), water and power management and safety governance systems (at the overlap of all 3 systems) and water distribution governance systems (at the overlap between natural and social systems).

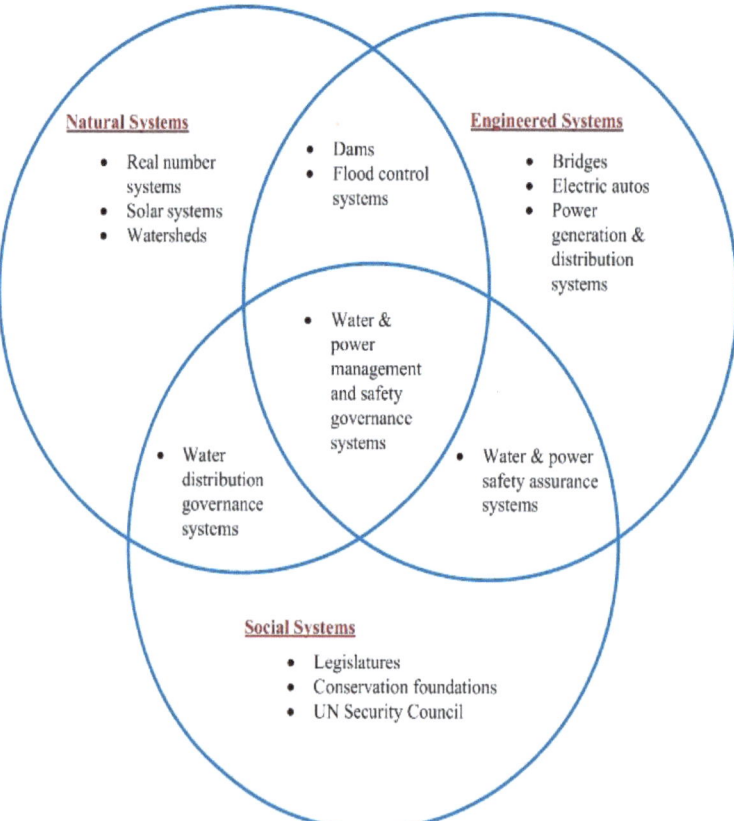

Figure 4 System boundaries of Engineered, Social and Natural systems
(Created using MS Visio 2007)

The use of modelling in each of these systems is exemplified in the following paragraphs.

A natural system - Modelling electron waves

When is a particle not a particle? This question became of intense interest following the publication in 1927 of a paper by Davisson and Germer (14) about the scattering of a beam of electrons which showed that electrons do not behave as solid particles, but rather like waves. Figure 5 shows the stripy affect that the electrons create on a screen when they have been fired through a pair of slits. This is not the clearly defined strips one would expect if the electrons behaved as particles.

In Cox and Forshaw's book on Quantum Mechanics (13) this wave-like behaviour is explained using the analogy of wave motion. If a wave is created and moves towards and through the slits it will form a stripy pattern on the screen akin to that of electrons. This means that electrons to be treated as waves have to be considered as having an infinite number of paths through the slits to create the stripy pattern. The wave analogy is further developed by studying the phases (peaks and troughs) of waves and how they reinforce or cancel one another out to create the interference pattern.

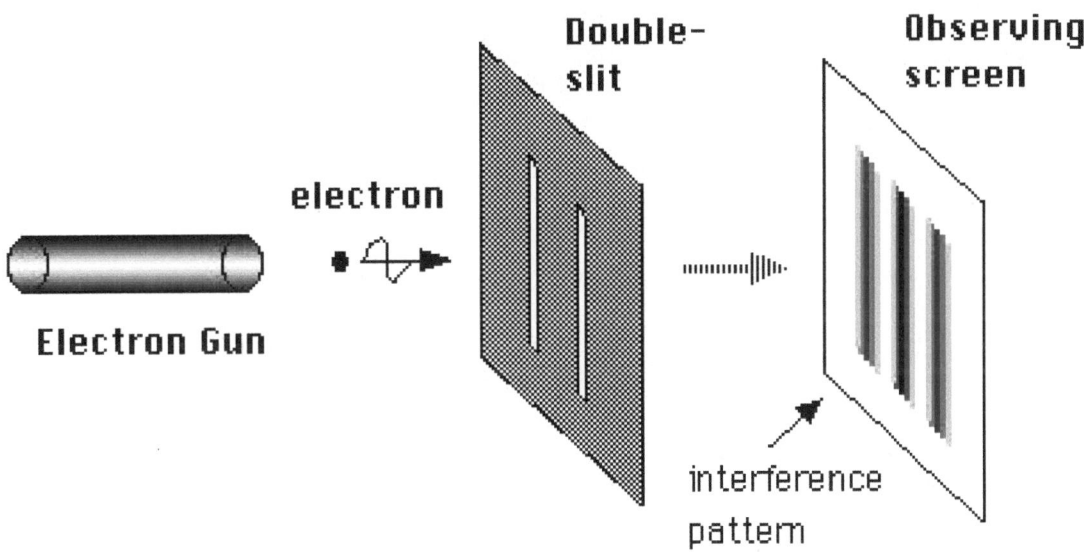

Figure 5 Stripy patterns as electrons pass through a pair of slits
(From https://en.wikipedia.org/wiki/Double-slit_experiment)

An engineered system - Modelling beam bridge construction

For this example, the structure of highway bridges is considered with the details drawn from the free encyclopaedia for UK steel construction information (15).

The majority of highway bridges are beam structures, either single spans or continuous spans, and composite bridges are of either multi-girder or ladder deck form.

The ladder deck construction typically has two main longitudinal members with the deck slab supported on cross girders that span transversely between the main girders - the slab then spans longitudinally between the cross girders. This arrangement is referred to as 'ladder deck' construction because the plan configuration of the steelwork, resembles the stringers and rungs of a ladder (see example in Figure 6a).

Figure 6a A ladder deck bridge at construction stage

Ladder decks can be modelled using computer-aided grillage analysis. The deck is idealized as a series of 'beam' elements (or grillages), connected and restrained at their joints. Each element is given an equivalent bending and torsional inertia to represent the portion of the deck which it replaces.

In the grillage model for a ladder deck (Figure 6b) the main longitudinal members represent full composite sections, intermediate longitudinal members represent slab only and transverse members will generally represent the composite section including cross-beams. Sometimes intermediate slab-only members may be included, in-between the composite transverse members.

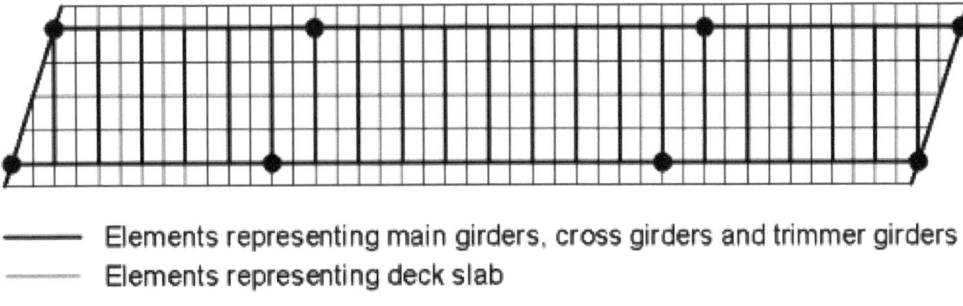

— Elements representing main girders, cross girders and trimmer girders
— Elements representing deck slab

Figure 6b Grillage model for a ladder deck bridge

A 3D model (Figure 6c) is likely to be required to model interaction between cross-girders and main girders, particularly the determination of 'U' frame stiffness and effects on cross-girders due to local application of special vehicles.

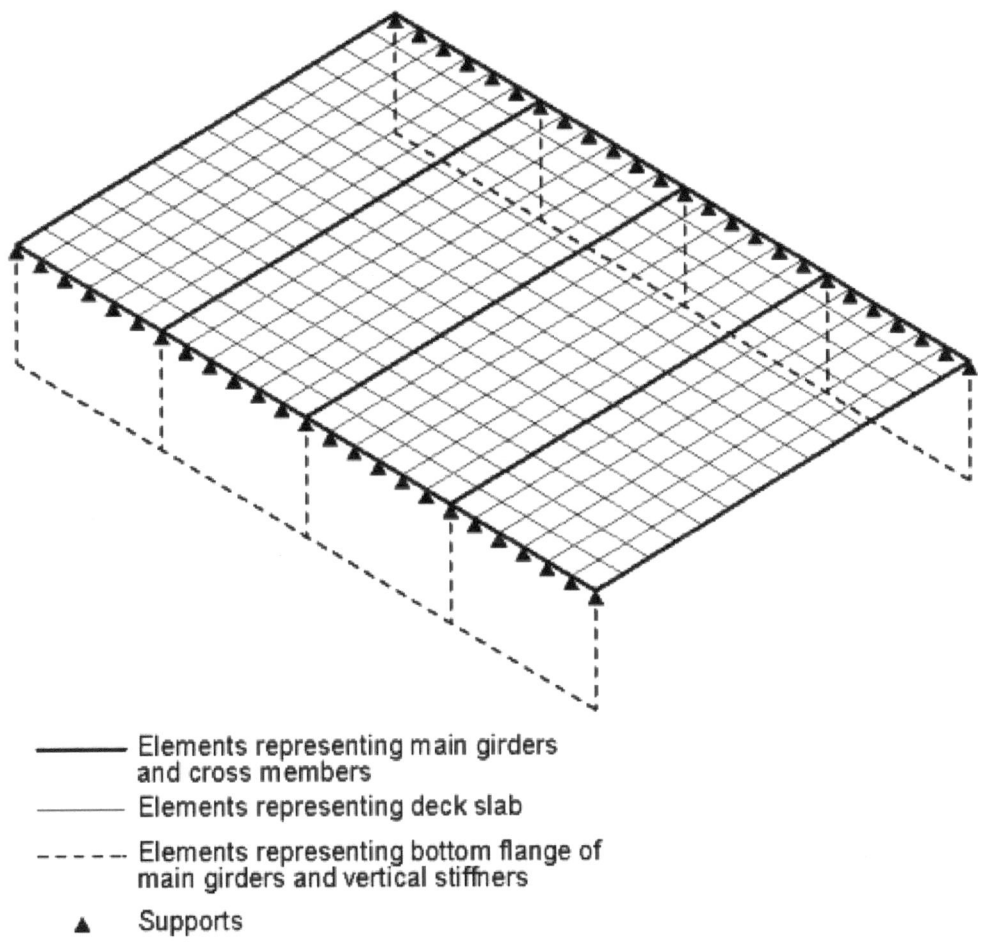

— Elements representing main girders and cross members
— Elements representing deck slab
----- Elements representing bottom flange of main girders and vertical stiffners
▲ Supports

Figure 6c Ladder deck 3D model for interaction of cross-girders and main girders

A social system - Modelling Galapagos social-ecological system

UNESCO added Galapagos to the list of World Heritage in Danger in 2007 and a study was commissioned (16) to provide new insights into the origins of the present-day crisis and suggest possible management alternatives. The Galapagos situation was examined from a broad systems perspective, conceptualizing the archipelago as a complex social-ecological system.

Based on the integrative analysis of Galapagos' social-ecological problems, three different plausible scenarios were modelled (Figure 7) and discussed with stakeholders, with tourism acting as the primary driver of change.

The endogenous model (safe-keeping of natural capital; 4A) revolves around a natural capital that is composed of healthy insular and marine ecosystems and generates a rich and varied flow of ecosystem services. The current situation of the archipelago was better described as a continentalized or exogenous model (consumption and stocking; 4B), which was poorly adjusted to the fragility, uniqueness, and particularities of the archipelago. The third scenario involving several loops of degradation, causes natural capital to reach a point at which it can no longer supply the high-quality sites needed for nature tourism (perverse model; 4C). In all three models, tourism acts as the primary indirect driver of change through its direct effects on other drivers like population growth (mostly from illegal immigration), movement of goods and services, and resource consumption.

The current tourism model was found to reduce the system's resilience through its effects on the economy, population growth, resource consumption, invasive species arrival, and lifestyle of the island residents. Opportunities to reorganize and maintain a desirable state did exist. However, strong political and management decisions were urgently needed to avoid an irreversible shift to a socially and environmentally undesirable regime.

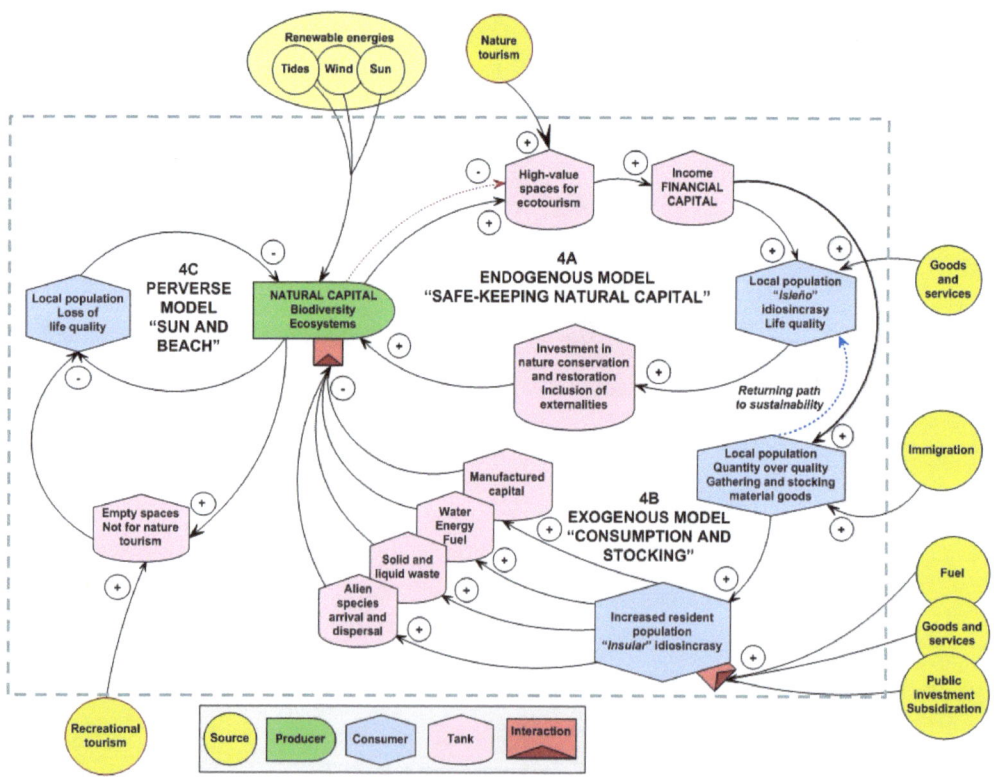

Figure 7 Simplified modelling of three plausible interconnected scenarios for the Galapagos social-ecological system, showing the tourism model as the main indirect driver of change

PROBLEM SOLVING METHODOLOGIES

A problem is *'doubtful or difficult matter; a matter that exercises the mind'*, a methodology is *'a body of methods used in a particular branch of study or activity'* and a method is *'a procedure for attaining an object'*. (1).

The definition of a problem is not restricted to those situations where you cannot proceed further with your thoughts due to some seemingly unresolvable conundrum. It also includes any condition where judgement of some kind needs to be made. Furthermore, problems can range from those where objectives can be clearly identified, progress is measured and implementation achieved to instances where situations are ill-structured and messy and end goals are ill-defined, if at all. The former has come to be termed 'hard' systems problems and the latter 'soft' systems problems (17), although problems may exhibit some characteristics of both.

This distinction gives rise to the different methodologies (hard and soft) used to address these problems within systems practice as is indicated in Figure 2 and Figure 3.

In relation to the types of system described above the modelling of a beam bridge can be considered an example of a hard system problem as the use of grillage analysis is well known and predicable in its outcome. In contrast the analysis of the Galapagos social-ecological system concerns a complex social system and produces an unpredictable result and hence falls more in the 'soft' problem category.

The examination of the behaviour of electron-waves uses a wave analogy to help describe the behaviour of electrons, the understanding of which had baffled scientists and has soft problem properties.

Hard System Methodologies

Hard system methodologies are systematic in their approach as they generally involve step-by-step procedures to achieve a predefined outcome. They evolved through the development of 'systems analysis', 'systems engineering' and 'operations research'.

Systems analysis has been defined in various ways, some specific to computerised systems, others indicating a more generalised application. Thus the International Standards Organisation in their Systems and Software Engineering standard (18) define it as *'A systematic investigation of a real or planned system to determine the information requirements and processes of the system and how these relate to each other and to any other system'*. More generally Checkland (19) describes it as 'the systematic appraisal of the costs and other implications of meeting a defined requirement in various ways'.

Systems analysis originated in the 1950s as part of a range of techniques developed by the RAND Corporation (20) to evaluate alternative nuclear weapons scenarios. Its success in the field of warfare led to wider application in government and social sciences.

A generalised representation of the systems analysis process is shown in Figure 8.

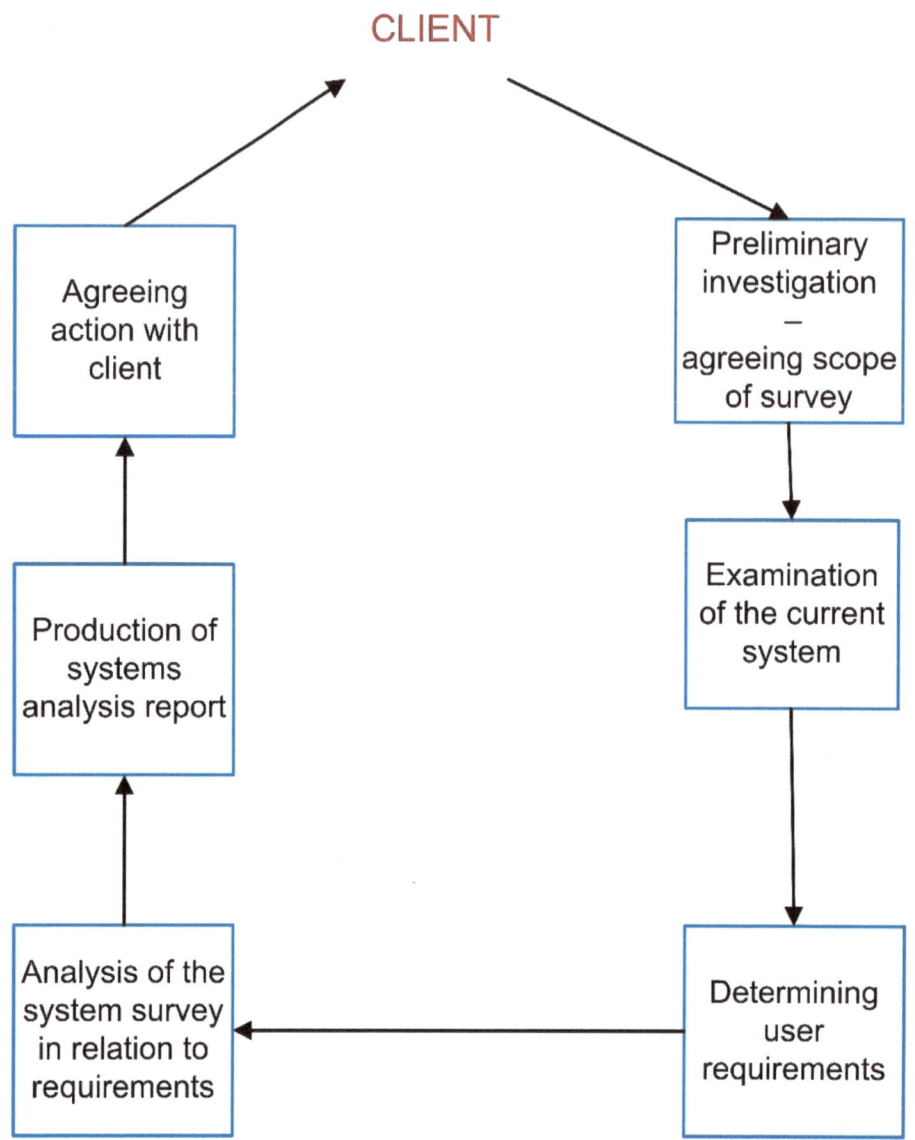

Figure 8 Generalised systems analysis processes
(Created using MS Visio 2007)

Systems engineering (SE) was developed primarily to manage large projects such as the design and development of the Intercontinental ballistic missile (ICBM). As with system analysis it is open to various definitions. Checkland (19) considers it to be a *'set of activities that together lead to the creation of a complex man-made entity and/or the procedures and information flows associated with its operation'*.

An alternative definition given by SEBoK (8) is *'Systems Engineering (SE) is an interdisciplinary approach and means to enable the realization of successful systems. It focuses on holistically and concurrently understanding stakeholder needs; exploring opportunities; documenting requirements; and synthesizing, verifying, validating, and evolving solutions while considering the complete problem, from system concept exploration through system disposal'*.

The International Council on Systems Engineering (INCOSE) consider that the SE process is usually comprised of the following seven tasks: State the problem, Investigate alternatives, Model the system, Integrate, Launch the system, Assess performance, and Re-evaluate. These functions can be summarized with the acronym SIMILAR: State, Investigate, Model, Integrate, Launch, Assess and Re-evaluate. This Systems Engineering process is shown in Figure 9. They emphasise that the process is not sequential as the functions are performed in a parallel and iterative manner.

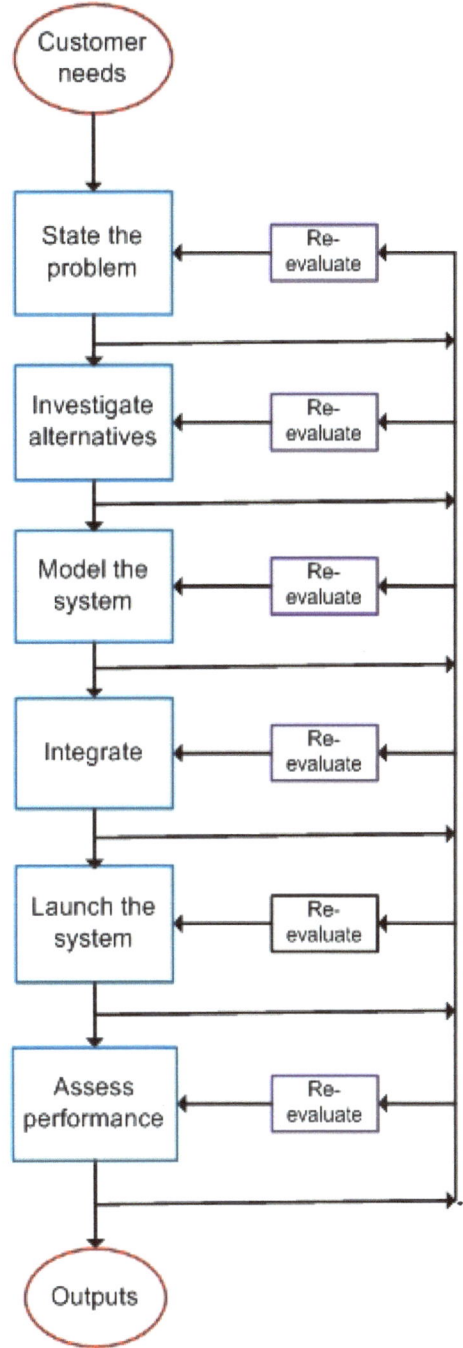

Figure 9 The SIMILAR tasks for Systems Engineering
(Created using MS Visio 2007)

Operations research (O.R.) - also known as operational research in the UK and sometimes termed as management science or industrial engineering - is defined as 'a discipline that deals with the application of advanced analytical methods to help make better decisions' (21)

Large OR projects typically require a model of the system, a way of valuing (estimating the value to us of) the outputs of the system, and a way of making decisions to improve that value (22).

Its application can draw on a wide range of techniques, many mathematical in nature. Examples are shown in Figure 10 and included in a list of techniques for business improvement available on my website.

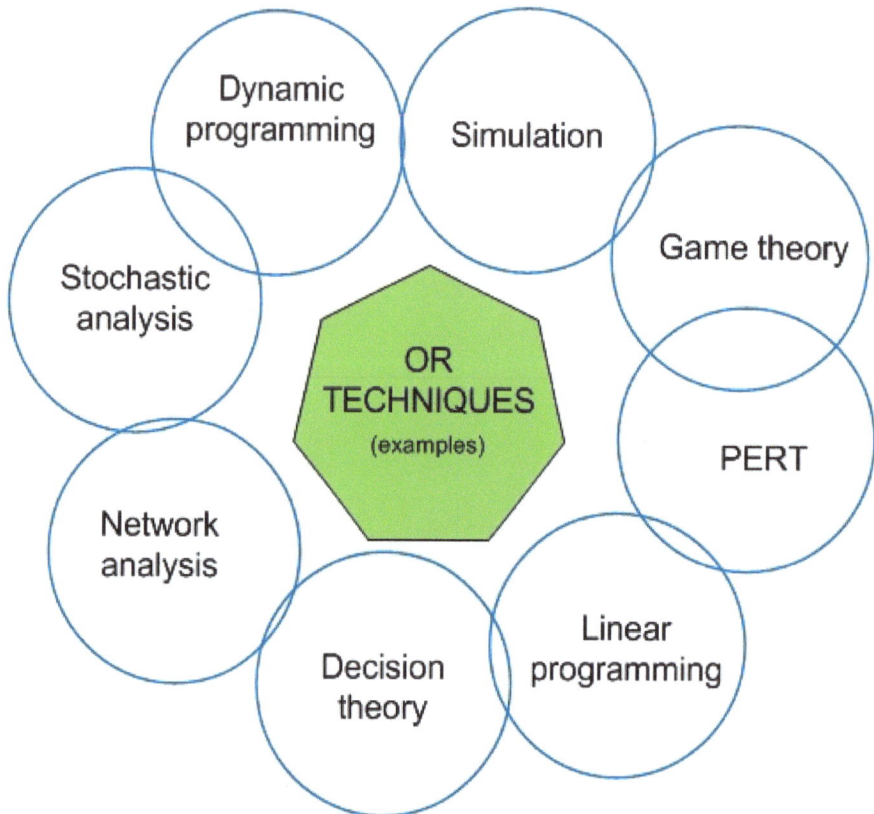

Figure 10 Examples of operations research techniques (Created using MS Visio 2007)

Soft System Methodologies

The focus of most problem-solving methods and methodologies is on objective and quantitative aspects to the detriment of subjective and qualitative issues. These latter may be the more important factors in deciding the success or otherwise of a project. This problem is compounded if, for example, there is uncertainty in the first place about what are the issues and concerns that need to be addressed. It is in this context of human activity systems that Checkland (17) provides the benchmark for a soft systems methodology (SSM).

An overview of SSM is provided in Figure 11 in which are depicted various stages, some being in the 'real world', others in the 'abstract world' of systems thinking.

Note that the kind of problems to which SSM might be applied could be classed as 'wicked' problems – a description applied in the context of 'issue and dialogue mapping' as considered later.

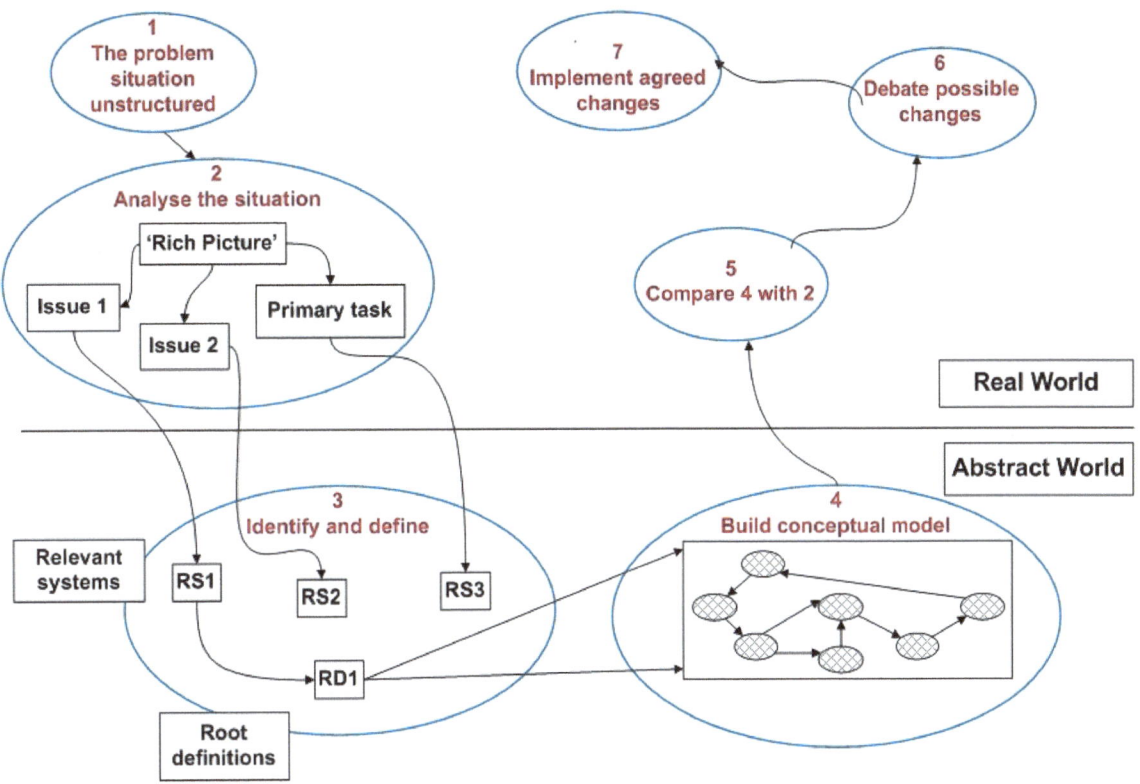

Figure 11 Stages of the soft systems methodology
(Created using MS Visio 2007)

The stages are usually undertaken iteratively rather than in series and comprise the following:

Stage 1 (Real World): The Problem Situation: Unstructured

The first stage involves recognition of a 'messy' situation, identifying elements of relatively slow-to-change structure and of continuously-changing process. It is important to avoid imposing a particular form to the situation; it is necessary to think about the roles of the client, problem-owner and problem-solver

Stage 2 (Real World): The Problem Situation: Expressed

Here a 'Rich Picture' (typically a hand drawn cartoon) is produced which incorporates 'hard' factual and 'soft' subjective information; structure and processes and their interaction; people and players involved; tensions and conflicts. The aim of the Rich Picture is to help identify new ways of viewing the situation and to extract Primary Tasks (these being tasks that the organisation in question was established to perform, or tasks which are essential for survival) and Issues (matters of concern or which are the subject of dispute). (An example of what could be considered a Rich Picture is depicted in the later discussions on Sketchnotes).

Stage 3 (Systems World): Relevant Systems and Root Definitions

Here the aim is not to identify what systems need to be engineered or improved, but rather what are the names of notional systems which from the analysis phase seem relevant to the problem. Having identified such systems, they are then defined more formally by way of Root Definitions (a concise, tightly constructed description of a human activity system which states what the system is).

Stage 4 (Systems World): Conceptual Models

A graphical model is built on the basis of the chosen Root Definition and comprises a structured set of activities expressed as verbs. They are justified purely on logical terms, not by mapping on to the real world.

Stage 5 (Real World): Comparison of Conceptual Model with Reality

Back in the real world one now looks for similarities and differences between the conceptual model from Stage 4 and the Real World situation from Stage 2; the results of the comparison are recorded and topics are identified for discussion

Stage 6 (Real World): Debate Feasible and Desirable Changes

A structured discussion is undertaken with those involved - e.g. client, problem-owner(s) and problem-solver(s) - with the aim of identifying ideas which are both systemically desirable and culturally feasible

Stage 7 (Real World): Implement Agreed Changes

Changes may involve changes in structure, procedures or in attitudes and are implemented if agreed.

It is recognised that the methodology does not provide explicit advice concerning implementation as the 'problem areas' that may be subject of study can be completely different in nature. Thus one problem may relate to human conflicts in an organisation, while another may be to identify the most suitable business area for piloting a new computer system. The actions that need to be taken following agreement at Stage 7 will therefore differ widely.

SSM is a well-established methodology and has had wide application across government and commerce. It is an assembly of principles applied at different stages, and it is perfectly possible to utilise parts of the process in isolation, such as drawing a Rich Picture to clarify issues, or formulating a Root Definition (RD) to firm up on the scope of a software development project. The intellectual process of devising a Root Definition is worth considering further.

Root Definitions

The Root Definition is a concise, tightly constructed description of a human activity system which states what the system is. It needs to contain certain elements these being:

Customer(s) of the system - those who will benefit (or be the victim of) the system's activities

Actor(s) - person(s) who carry out one or more of the activities in the system

Transformation - this is the key feature of the definition and refers to the core transformation process of the human activity system, i.e. the process of converting input(s) into output(s)

Weltanchaunung (or World view) - the unquestioned image of model or the world which makes the particular human activity system a meaningful one to consider

Owner(s) of the system - those who have sufficient power over the system to cause its demise

Environment - constraints which the system has to take as given

The initial letters of these elements form the mnemonic CATWOE to identify these six crucial characteristics which should be included in a well-formulated Root Definition.

To demonstrate its use, the following Root Definition (RD) is based on the results from a study of the UK personal tax system (23).

'A system to give staff access to a single, coherent, summary record of taxpayers' affairs by providing a single IT interface which accesses all Revenue records for an individual, presenting that information in a single view and allowing single edit revisions to those records. [i.e. A system in which, when data is updated on one record, the relevant changes are reflected in all the records holding that data rather than each record having to be updated individually] to enhance customer service, provide proactive advice to taxpayers, improve efficiency and, over time lead to more reliable, up-to-date records.'

Analysing the RD using CATWOE indicates:

Customer(s) - Staff and individuals

Actor(s) - Inland Revenue and its IT partners

Transformation - Takes and updates information from different systems and presents it in coherent ways

Weltanschauung - It would allow staff to operate more efficiently, would improve customer service. Further, treating an individual's tax affairs as a single entity is a good thing. The change could also lead to a paperless office and may improve compliance.

Owner(s) - Inland Revenue

Environment - the IT resources available, the legislation on data sharing and resources to run such a system

Comparison of hard and soft methodologies

As mentioned earlier it is possible and often beneficial to combine the use of different methodologies to achieve a useful outcome. This was the case of the aforementioned study of the UK personal tax system (23) which used a combination of a hard system operational research (OR) approach using data mining and a Checkland-based soft systems methodology (SSM). Here the soft systems approach was not used at the outcome to clarify the situation so that a hard problem solving solution could then be applied. Instead, and consciously, the two approaches were intertwined.

The data mining elements involved basic data analysis, web-link analysis and cluster analysis. The SSM was employed as an overarching methodological guide and to gain an understanding of how different stakeholders regard the UK's personal tax system. Both approaches contributed to problem structuring and played a part in detailed analysis. A comparison of hard and soft is provided in (Figure 12).

	Hard Systems approach	**Soft Systems approach**
Assumption	The world contains systems that can be engineered.	The world is problematical but can be explored intellectually with systems.
Methodology	Oriented to goal seeking, optimisation and prediction.	Oriented to learning, exploration and commitment
Information input	From a source that is defensibly there in the world, with an agreed or shared meaning, observer independent.	Based on judgement, opinion, some ambiguity, observer dependent.
Modelling	System models are models of the real world (ontologies).	System models are intellectual conceptual constructs (epistemologies).
Validity	Repeatable and comparable with the real world in some sense.	Defensibly coherent, logically consistent, plausible.
Outcome	Talks the language of 'solutions'.	Talks the language of 'issues'.

Figure 12 Comparison of hard and soft methodologies

STANDARDISED MODELLING METHODS

The range of available modelling techniques and support software is vast and continues to grow driven by the types of problem addressed, the intellectual rigour applied to formalize the thinking behind the methods and developments in technology.

The ability rapidly to sketch on the back of an envelope will never be fully replaced by technology and may be the first instance that some visual record is made relating to some troubling matter. Although later, downstream, there may be some formalized methodology or tailored modelling tool that can be usefully applied to what is now recognised as a problem, these early deliberations are more likely to rely on broadly-applicable software of which there are many to choose from. The design of some modelling methods has drawn on theoretical and scientific studies in education, cognitive psychology or the work place, others have developed simply from an understanding of what proves useful.

As a way to address the wide range of approaches on offer, the subject is first discussed from the viewpoint of those modelling methods that rely on some means of formalization or standardization as regards underlying coding, notations and linkages, for example. In this grouping are included Universal Modelling Language (UML), data modelling and Business Process Model and Notation (BPMN). More generally applicable methods follow thereafter.

Universal Modelling Language (UML)

The Universal Modelling Language is a graphical modelling language that was developed to standardise different notational systems and help in describing and designing software. It was adopted as a standard in 1997 for object-oriented modelling by the Object Management Group (OMG) which is responsible for its onward management (24). Version 2.5.1 of the document specifying UML (25) runs to over 700 pages, so its use is not for the faint-hearted.

The set of UML diagram types can be divided into those concerned with structure and behaviour as shown in Figure 13. Structure relates to such factors as the attributes and connectivity of the object under consideration while behaviour is to do with the processes or operations that it undergoes. In UML an object is one that combines both structure and behaviour.

Despite the large number of publications relating to UML and the promotional efforts of the OMG there is little evidence that it has extensive use outside of academia and the IT and software community. Even there the specification is not used in its entirety.

The use made of UML has been characterized by Fowler (26) as - sketch, blueprint and programming language - with the first usage mode arguably being the most common. Sketching can be used at the outset of a project to help developers communicate key aspects of the intended system, or can be applied to existing software code to help understand how it works (the former can be termed 'forward engineering', the latter 'reverse engineering'). Sketches only require the use of the simpler UML model notations which can often be created by diagramming tools that form part of office software packages. Note that the word 'sketch' appears later in 'Sketchnotes' in a somewhat different context, although such 'notes' could be used in a UML environment.

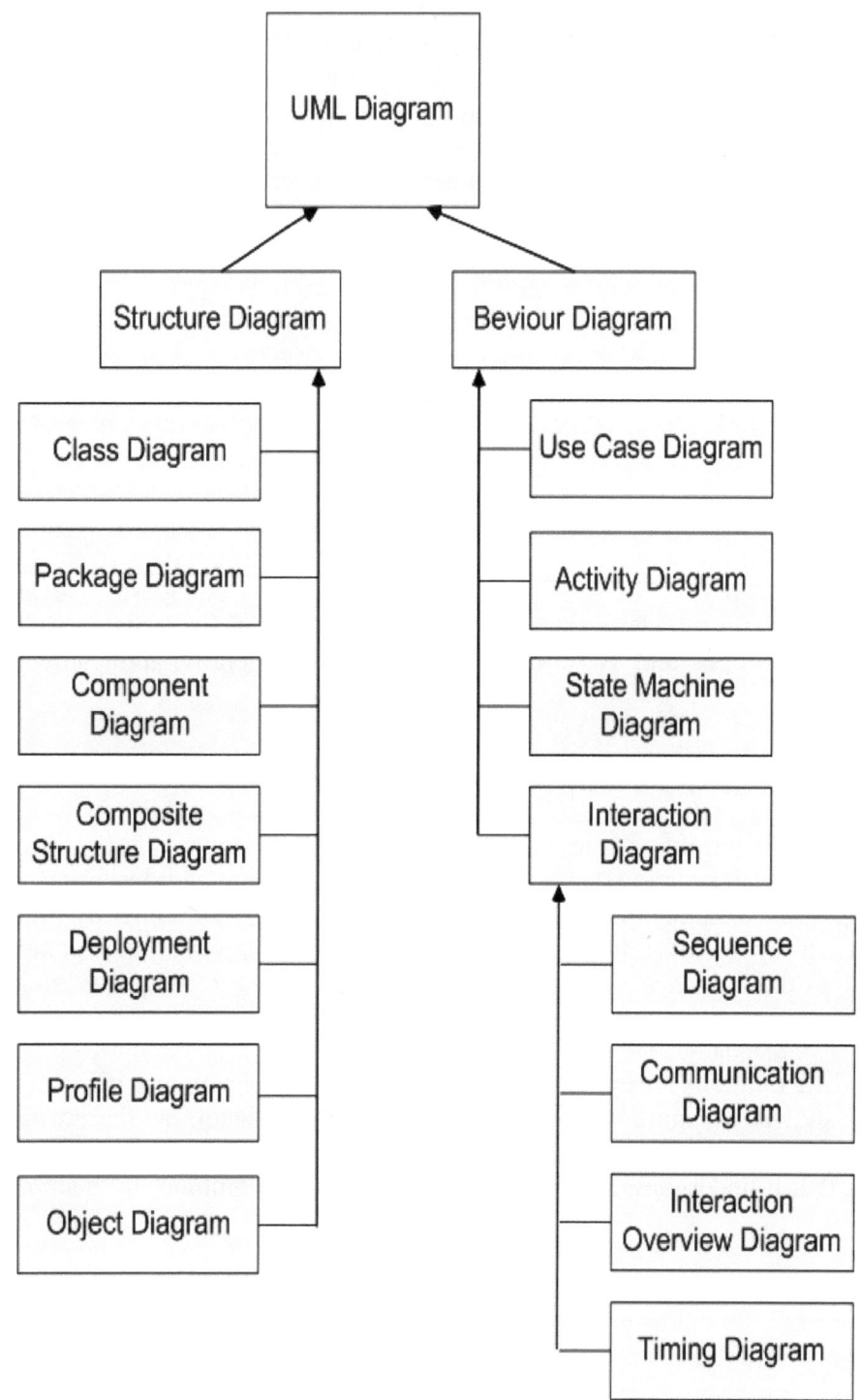

Figure 13 UML Diagram Types (Created using MS Visio 2007)

Blueprints are designs in sufficient details for a programmer to write software code. They will make use of a wider selection of UML diagrams and require the use of specialised tools often referred to (more in past perhaps) as CASE - computer-aided software engineering - tools.

UML used for programming has developers drawing UML diagrams that can be compiled directly into executable code. Fowler views UML use as a programming language as a 'nice idea', but doubts that it will ever see significant usage.

A small survey (27) of IT professionals undertaken in 2013 with 162 respondents, showed that while 13% found UML useful, 45% of respondents could get away without using it; see Figure 14. Ambler elsewhere bemoans the complexity of UML and the tendency to add more types of diagram at each iteration of the Specification (28).

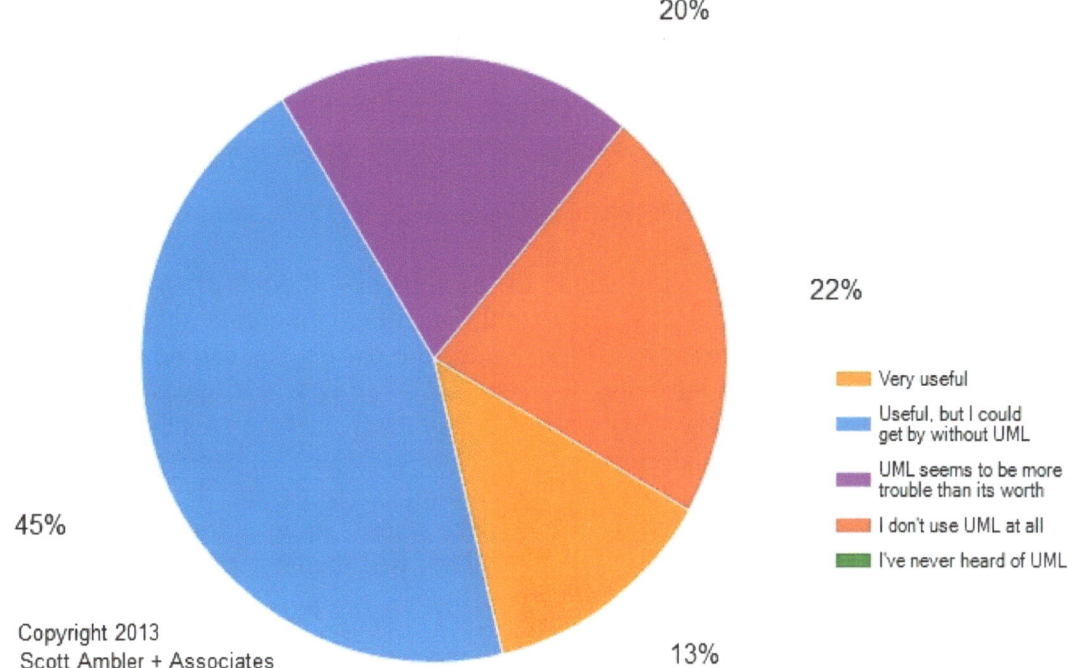

Figure 14 What people think of UML (27)

Newcomers to UML are generally recommended to focus on the simpler forms of class and sequence diagrams as these are likely to prove the most useful and are also more widely used. Figure 15 indicates the popularity of the various diagrams from the previously mentioned survey, including one for BPMN (Business Process Model and Notation) which technique is considered later. The two UML diagrams which will be considered here are class diagrams and sequence diagrams. Use cases are dealt with later in the context of business process modelling using BPMN.

Class diagrams are models to describe objects. An object is a concept or something with identity that has meaning for some use or application; examples range from a person or car to an event or place. Objects are at the heart of object oriented (OO) system software development.

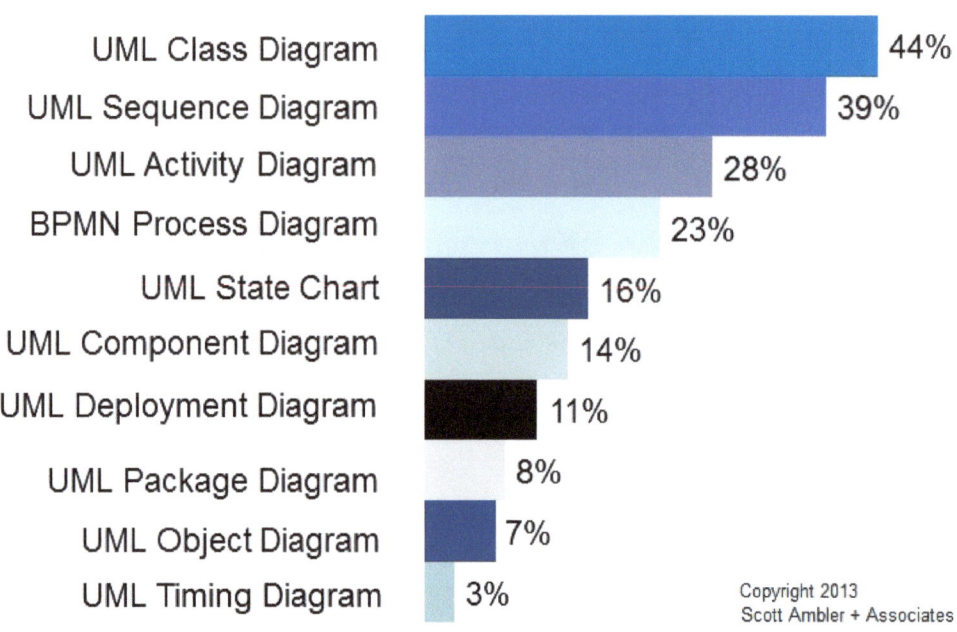

Figure 15 UML/BPMN usage in general (27)

If we consider 'car objects', these will include the various new models from Mercedes, Renault, Honda and other manufacturers and the multitude of existing individually-owned cars on the road. Despite the differences in appearance the car objects can be abstracted into a 'car class' having common attributes such engine, steering wheel, gears, seats etc. Similarly, there can be a 'bicycle class' with its own abstracted attributes. Each such class describes a possibly infinite set of individual objects.

A class diagram, however, does not only describe these static attributes, it also encapsulates dynamic properties which, for the car class, will include operations such as movement, gear shift and maintenance.

As an example a class model for a customer order as dealt with by a supplier is shown in Figure 16.

The boxes are classes, each with three sections; the top one containing the name of the class, the central one the attributes (properties) of the class and the final one the operations it undergoes (details of the latter can be omitted in conceptual-level models which are discussed later). The attributes shown for the 'Order' class are the date it was received, the order number provided by the customer, the price (value) of the order and an indication of whether customer has made a prepayment. The operations undertaken relating to the order are despatching the order and formally closing the order once it has been completed. (Note the convention that the class name, if consisting of more than one word, is written 'joined up' in so called camel writing - thus 'OrderDetail').

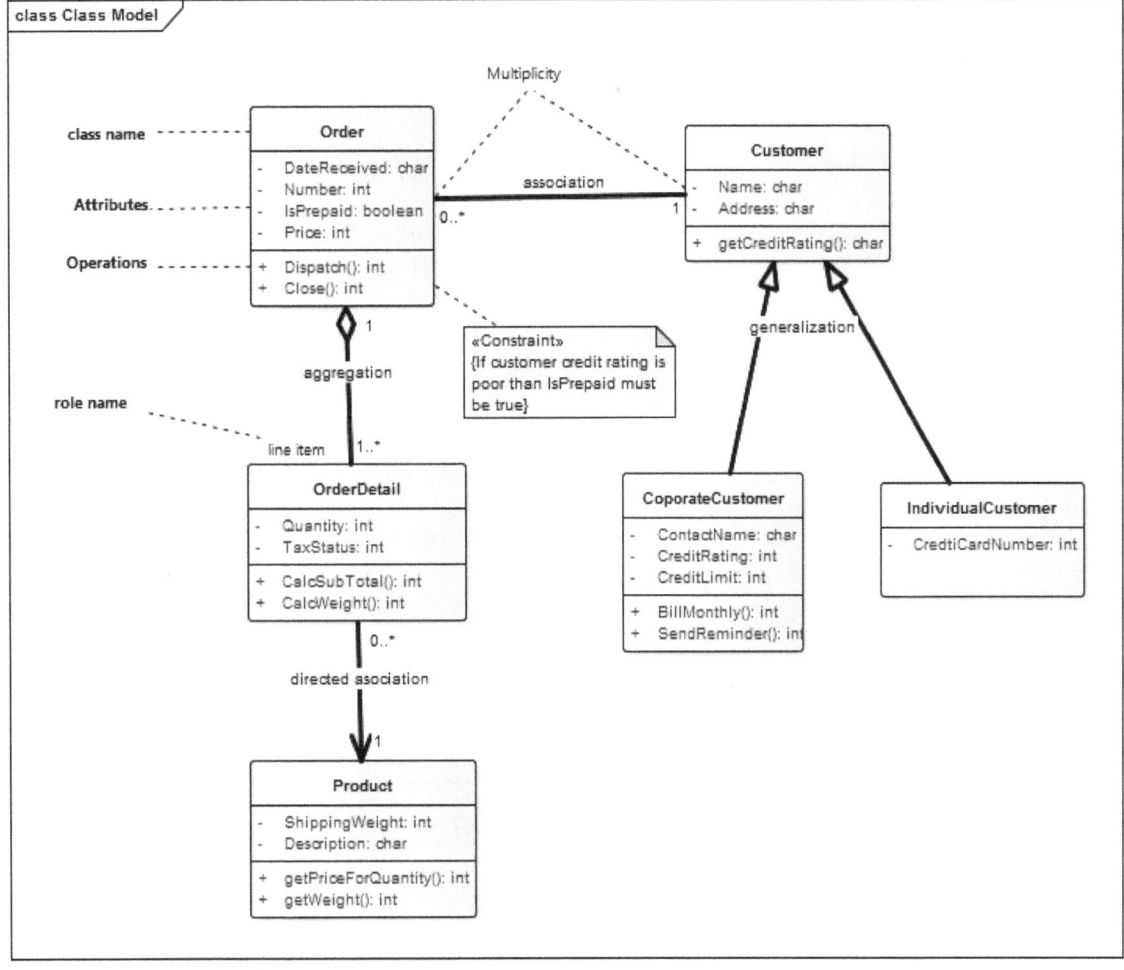

Figure 16 Class model for a customer order
(Created using Enterprise Architect from Sparx Systems
http://www.sparxsystems.com/products/ea/index.html)

The class diagram has three kinds of relationships:

Association - a relationship between two classes shown as a solid line. The line may be provided with arrowheads to indicate directionality of the relationship, as shown between 'OrderDetail' and 'Product' classes. An association has two ends. An end may have a role name to clarify the nature of the association. Thus an 'OrderDetail' is a line item of an 'Order'.

Aggregation - an association in which one class belongs to a collection, shown with an unfilled diamond end pointing to the part containing the whole. In the diagram 'Order' has a collection of 'OrderDetails' (line items).

Generalization - an inheritance link indicating one class is a super class of the other; shown as a triangle pointing to the superclass. 'Customer' is a superclass of 'CorporateCustomer' and 'IndividualCustomer' classes.

A navigability arrow on an association shows which direction the association can be traversed or queried. An 'OrderDetail' can be queried about a 'Product', but not the other way round. The arrows also indicate who 'owns' the association's implementation; in this case 'OrderDetail' has a 'Product'. Associations with no navigability arrows are bidirectional.

The **multiplicity** (or cardinality) of an association end is the number of possible instances of the class associated with a single instance of the other end. Multiplicities are single numbers or ranges of numbers. Those shown in the example are:

1 Meaning an 'Order' must have exactly one 'Customer'.

1..* Meaning an 'Order' must have at least one 'OrderDetail' (line item), but there is no upper limit as regards the number of line items in an 'Order'.

0..* Meaning a 'Customer' may not actually place an 'Order' but there is no upper limit as to the number of orders they may place.

Although there can only be one 'Customer' for each 'Order', a 'Customer' can generate any number of 'Orders'. This form of **constraint** defined by the interrelationships between association, attribute and generalization cannot, however, define every required constraint. The diagram shows a constraint concerning the credit rating of a customer. Such constraints can be defined in many ways in UML but must always appear inside the brackets {}.

Sequence diagrams are a form of interaction diagram and depict how groups of objects interact over time and show the messages that flow between them. They are useful for showing how objects communicate with other objects, and what messages trigger those communications. They are, however, not suitable for complex procedural logic. Figure 17 shows how the order shown in Figure 16 might be processed.

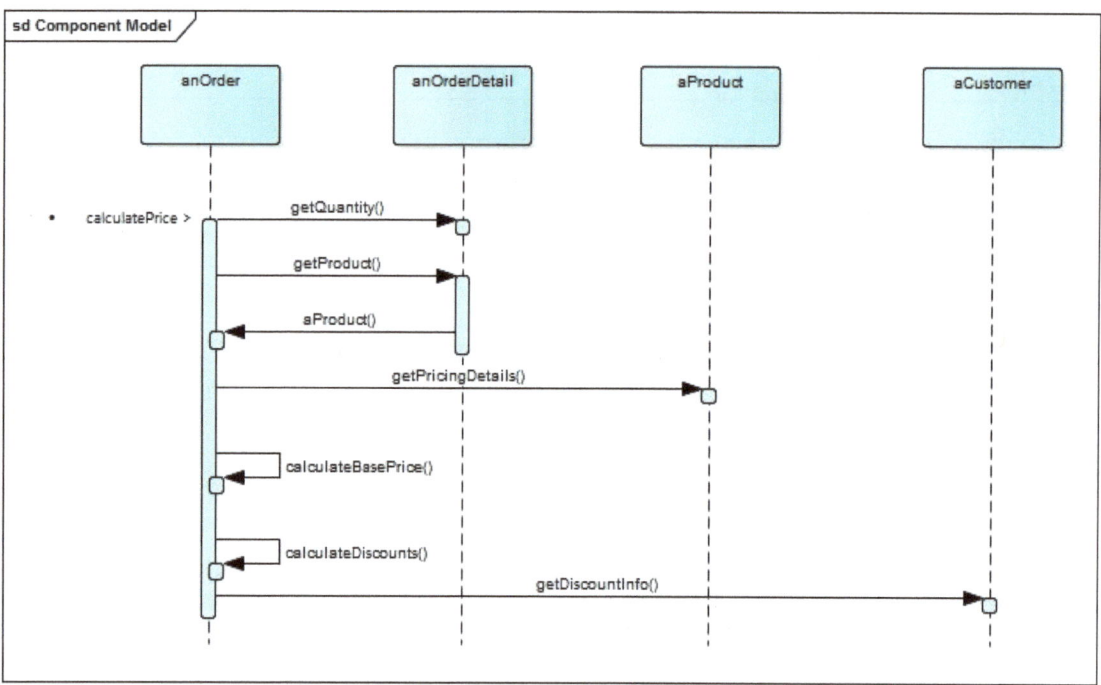

Figure 17 Sequence model for a customer order (Created using Enterprise Architect)

The boxes along the top are the 'participants', the vertical dashed lines are the 'lifelines' and the elongated boxes on the lifelines are 'activation boxes'. The arrowed lines represent the messages between participants. The process of dealing with an order progresses down the lifelines starting with:

- the Order sending 'getQuantity' and 'getProduct' messages to the 'OrderDetail';

- 'getPricingDetails' are obtained from the 'Product'.

- 'calculateBasePrice' and 'calculateDiscounts' are self-calls on the 'Order' enabling a 'getDiscountInfo' message to be sent to an instance of the customer.

There is much more to class and sequence diagrams (and UML) than can be covered here; see the Resources List for further information.

Data Modelling

A data model provides a graphical representation of the entities that are of importance to the matter under consideration and may show in great detail how they relate to one another. In an organizational context this may relate to its management or its business requirements.

Unlike object-oriented modelling using UML, data modelling is not concerned with behaviour or process but solely with structure and relationships. One can say that data (i.e. entity) models are used by the database designer to design a customer database while the (UML) class model is used by the software designer to define how the customer ordering process is to be implemented.

In the views of some practitioners (29) it is considered unfortunate that UML does not cater for data modelling, although some of its notations, particularly class diagrams, may be applied in restricted form.

Data can be considered to be elemental information given that virtually all recorded information is available in some electronic form or another. In the context of this Viewpoint 'Information' embraces that which is:

Structured: data, facts and figures in some organized form; those that are alike are grouped together and have defined format and length; similar ones have formal relationships to one another and
Unstructured: data that can be of any type and does not necessarily follow any defined format, sequence or rules. It can be considered as the direct product of human communication (see Figure 18).

At the beginning of the modelling process the analyst is faced with the real information world of the business from which they need to abstract the key information elements to gain some concept of what is relevant to the particular objective. This is recorded in the 'conceptual model' showing the broad relationships between the data and possibly identifying some significant attributes to supplement the definition of entities.

A conceptual model is often created as the precursor to a 'logical data model' (LDM). The LDM provides a more detailed graphical representation of an organization's business requirements. It contains the entities of importance to the organization and how they relate to one another and provides definitions and examples.

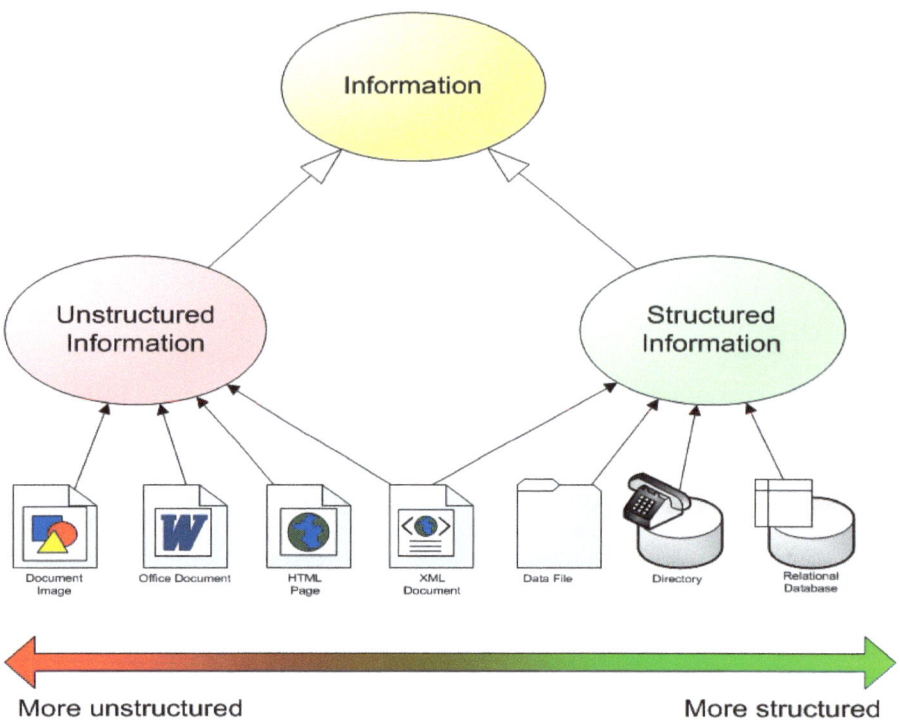

Figure 18 Structured and unstructured information
(Created using MS Visio 2007)

Thereby the LDM helps provide a common understanding and confirmation of business requirements. It gathers metadata (attributes that the entities possess) and facilitates its re-use and sharing and also facilitates business process improvement while decreasing development and maintenance time and cost.

Neither type of model takes any account of how the data might be organized physically in the production system, for example in a relational database. This is important as the data needs to be modelled in a way that reflects the logic of the business requirements and can be discussed with the business. The logical model design (schema) must not be constrained by how the logical system will be implemented, but it does form the basis for the physical database design.

Hence a succession of models – conceptual, logical and physical – can be used throughout the process as shown in Figure 19.

As an example from which to produce a logical data model, consider the purchase orders shown in Figure 20

Before modelling is undertaken it is important to analyse the data contained in these purchase orders to help identify and define the data needed to support the purchase order process and to inform the design of any intended software applications. The aim is to render the model more amenable to change such as the addition or elimination of entities and relationships and also to reduce redundancy of data. This element of the analysis is called 'data normalization' and is explained in Annex A.

The outcome of this normalization process leads to the entity relationship diagram in Figure 21.

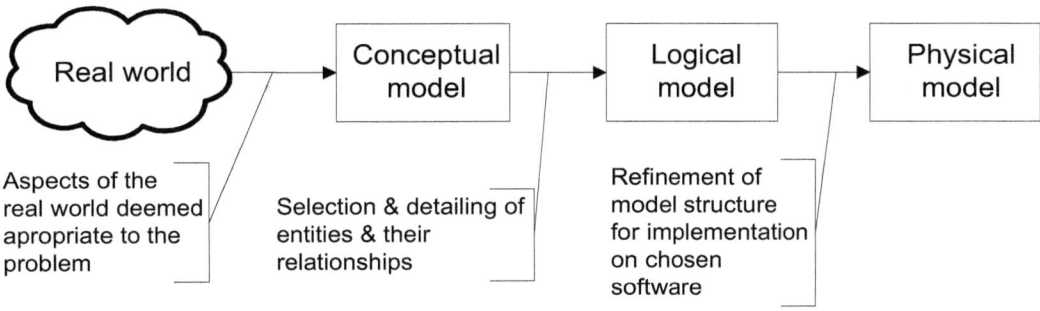

figure 19 Types of data model (Created using MS Visio 2007)

Order Number	1023		
Supplier Number	500106		
Supplier Name	J. Smith and Sons		
Supplier Address	14 High Street, Burgess Hill, RH16 2BA		
Order Date	25/07/10		
Delivery Date	31/08/10		
Part Number	Part Description	Quantity ordered	Price £
0463	Hook	150	15.00
1492	Line	1000	10.00
3164	Sinker	10	5.00
		Total	30.00

Order Number	1024		
Supplier Number	500106		
Supplier Name	J. Smith and Sons		
Supplier Address	14 High Street, Burgess Hill, RH16 2BA		
Order Date	25/08/10		
Delivery Date	31/09/10		
Part Number	Part Description	Quantity ordered	Price £
0463	Hook	75	7.50
1492	Line	500	5.00
3164	Sinker	100	50.00
		Total	62.50

Figure 20 Purchase order example

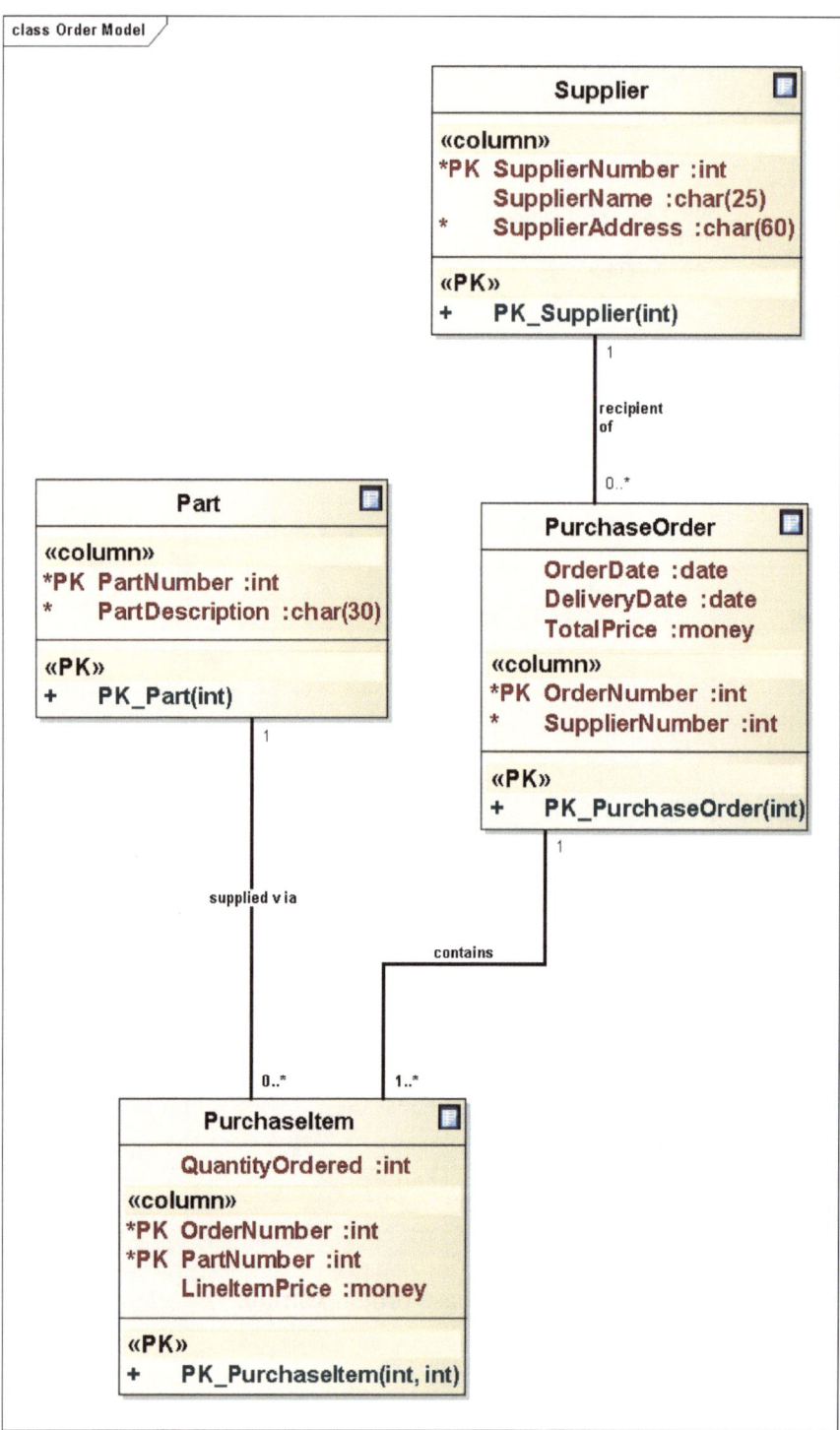

Figure 21 Entity relationship diagram of the purchase order (Created using Enterprise Architect from Sparx Systems)

Entity relationship diagrams in data modelling are similar to Class diagrams in UML, but on inspection similarities and differences are exposed.

Entities are shown as boxes and are always named in the singular at the top the box. These boxes are drawn in a form – a table indicating columns - that can render them acceptable for populating a relational database. Entities map directly to so-called persistent classes in an object model.

Attributes (as in UML) are named in the second row of the box. Each attribute has after its name an indication of the type of data, for example SupplierNumber is an integer, DeliveryDate is a date, TotalPrice is money and SupplierAddress holds characters with the allowed length noted in brackets. This enables a database to handle the data correctly.

Every entity must have at least one attribute that can be used to uniquely identify the entity. This is known as the entity's primary key(s). Attributes may be either part of the primary key (PK), mandatory or optional. These key attributes appear in the bottom row of the boxes. Some attributes comprise standard list of terms (standing data) which form 'pick lists' from which appropriate terms are selected. Thus there could be an additional entity 'PartType' linked to the entity 'Part' to classify them according to some agreed criteria, for example type of material from which parts are made.

Relationships are lines joining the entities with associated wording to clarify the relationship. The multiplicity at each end of the relationship uses the same conventions as explained earlier for class diagrams.

1 = one and only one (mandatory association)

0…* = zero or more (optional at the zero at the end of a relationship indicates it may not apply)

1…* = one or more (mandatory)

0…1 = zero or one (optional)

For example, each PurchaseOrder can only have one Supplier, but a supplier may be the recipient of no PurchaseOrder, or one or more orders. Hence it is possible to maintain a list of suppliers and their addresses even though some of them have not received an order. Similarly, a Part may be part of a PurchaseItem and it is possible to maintain a list of parts some of which have not been ordered. However, a PurchaseItem must relate to only one part.

Data Model Templates
Identifying relevant data and understanding its structure and relationships are key to the success of building a business system. While the procedures that are followed to process a purchase order from placement to receipt of goods, for example, may vary from one organization to another, there will be considerable commonality in the data attributes used e.g. order number, supplier identifier and order date.

Instead it 'reinventing the wheel' use can be made of standard data model templates available from a range of sources to cover not just the ubiquitous order processing, but more specialised areas within specific industries such as banking, aircraft and pharmaceutical. These standard data models (30) may have been agreed between those in the same industry, through international standards organizations or via the work of software system vendors for example.

Searching on the internet using 'data model examples' or some similar search phrase will find some that can provide a useful starting point and save unnecessary effort - see Resources List for example sources.

Business Process Model and Notation (BPMN)

BPMN is a graphical notation for specifying business processes in a business process diagram using a standard notation. It aims to be comprehensible to business users yet provide complex process semantics for technical users enabling, at the extreme, platform-independent interoperability and a basis for reliable communication between different stakeholders. It was developed by the Business Process Management Initiative (BPMI) which subsequently merged with the Object Management Group who is now responsible for its maintenance and the BPMN standard (31) which amounts to over 500 pages.

Figure 22 depicts a simple order fulfilment process where the process boxes, flow lines and decision box diamonds are familiar to anyone who has used traditional flow charts.

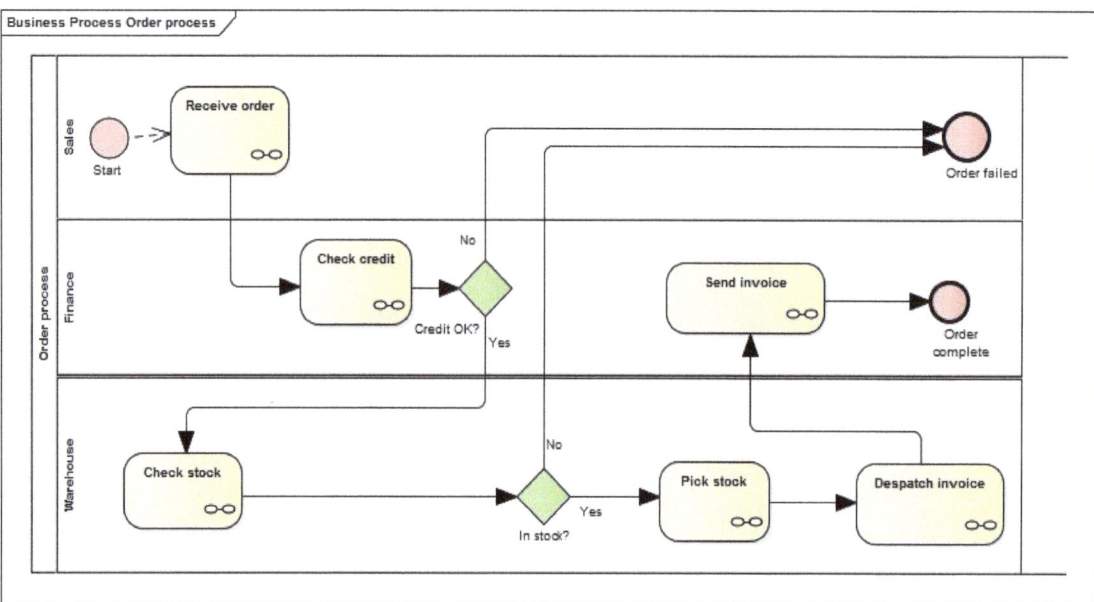

Figure 22 A BPMN diagram of an order process (Created using Enterprise Architect)

The BPMN contains a rich set of graphical notations as shown in Figure 23 with process logic being based around three main elements - activities, gateways and events.

Participants in the process are delineated in 'lanes' with the information flows passing between them shown as solid arrow connectors.

Activity is a unit of work with a clear beginning and end and represented by a rounded rectangle. (A Task represents an atomic Activity included within a Process. Libraries of tasks can be stored for reuse).

Process is a sequence of activities whose start is triggered by an event.

Event is something that occurs during the running of a process, for example a customer cancels an order currently being processed.

Gateway conditions may apply which when applied direct the flow in one or another direction. They comprise diamond-shaped notations with labels indicating the logic to be applied.

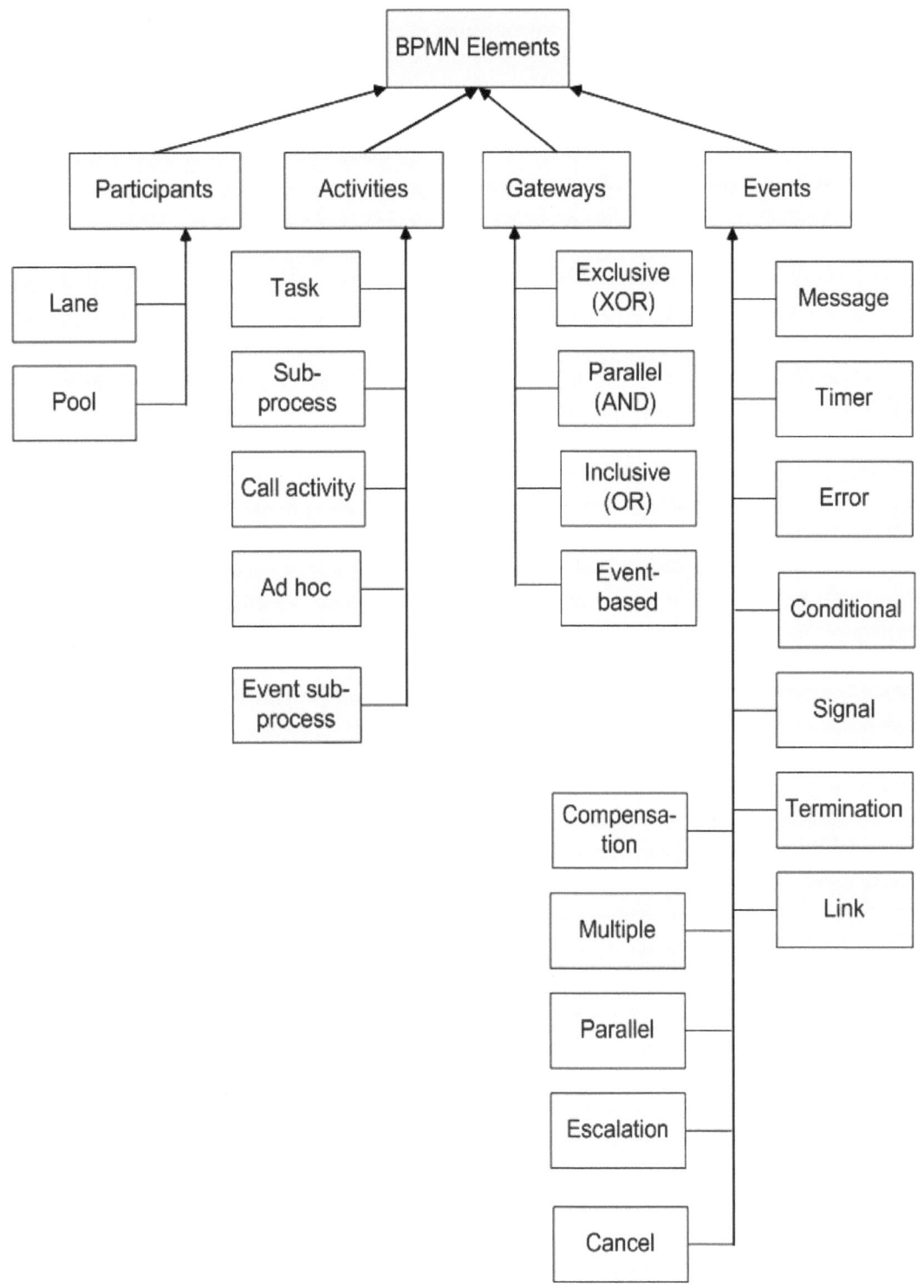

Figure 23 Types of graphical notations used in BPMN (Created using MS Visio 2007)

BPMN (like UML) has an advantage over ad hoc graphical charting approaches of being a standard maintained by an organisation, OMG, independent of hardware suppliers and software vendors. Although those producing BPMN (and UML) tools may differ somewhat in how they implement the standards at least business users and those from IT do have recourse to a single authoritative source of information that can foster dialogue between them.

However as with UML, BPMN is not without its critics (32) (33) some of the deficiencies claimed being:

- A failure as a basis for reliable communication of business process models between different stakeholders (e.g. processes defined by non-technical people using BPMN are not usable AS-IS without further technical work),

- Ambiguities in some of the descriptions and under-specifications in concepts leading to incompatible interpretations in design, analysis and use of business processes, and (arguably the most significant)

- A failure to deliver interoperability between different technical platforms (e.g. a model produced on one platform cannot be reused without intervention).

For those starting out on business process analysis BPMN is not necessarily the first choice of diagramming tool. This is due to the time and effort needed to learn the complexities of the product and the fact that the diagrams produced are not necessarily readily comprehensible to the business client. Simpler, more generic diagramming software might be more appropriate, many types of which are covered in the Modelling Techniques chapter.

Before leaving the topic of process modelling mention should be made of Use Case diagrams which are one of the UML behaviour diagrams shown previously in Figure 13 and are another way to represent processes within a system.

Use Cases

Use cases capture the interaction between 'actors' and the system being studied. Actors can be a human user, a machine, or even another system or subsystem. Use cases describe a scenario (a sequence of steps describing an interaction between a user and the system) which can be represented as text or as a model. A use case model may comprise several use case diagrams (or descriptions), these being one of the standard UML notations.

There are different flavours and levels of use cases; one may be focused on an interaction with the business, another with the software system while some will take high level views of the situation and others will address the finer detail.

Taking the example of processing an order in Figure 22, the use case could be documented as shown in Figure 24. To deal with the conditions in Figure 22 (is the customer credit worthy and is item in stock) use is made of 'extensions' that describe the condition to be satisfied. The extension is started by naming the step at which the condition is detected and provides a short description of the condition.

Alternatively, the use case can be represented as a diagram as in Figure 25. The three actors - sales, warehouse and finance - are shown interacting with the system. The conditions, checking credit worthiness and availability of stock, are shown with 'include' relationships which implies that the included behaviour is a necessary part of the system.

PROCESS AN ORDER

Main Success Scenario
1. Sales receives the order
2. Sales confirms credit worthiness
3. Warehouse checks stocks
4. Warehouse picks stock
5. Warehouse despatches invoice (to finance)
6. Finance sends invoice to customer

Extensions
2a: System fails to confirm credit worthiness
    2a.1: Order is cancelled
4a: Warehouse fails to find stock
    4a.1: Order is cancelled

Figure 24 Use case text for process an order

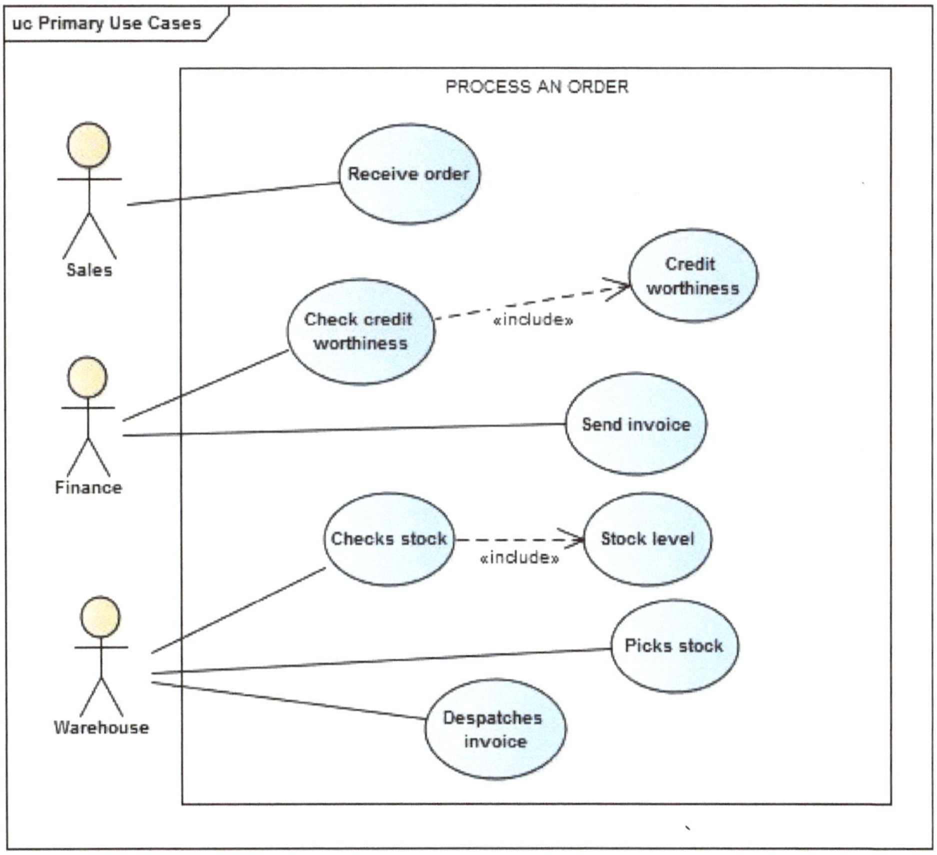

Figure 25 Use case diagram for process an order
(created using Enterprise Architect from Sparx Systems)

Use cases are best adopted (if at all) to obtain an early view of the system under consideration. They provide an external viewpoint and are not associated with any classes within the system. It is too easy to become obsessed with producing diagrams and end up going nowhere. Text versions of use cases are easier to produce and will almost certainly be more readily comprehended. Each such use case can, if needed, form the basis for producing process models based, for example on BPMN notations.

The relationship between data analysis and process analysis

The approaches to process modelling and data modelling have so far been considered in isolation. However, in real life data analysis and process analysis should go hand-in-hand, but need not be undertaken simultaneously or in any particular order. If process analysis is undertaken first it may generate local data and process models for each functional area. The individual data models can then be combined to create an initial global data model.

Note that a functional area is not necessarily the same as a business area in the management structure as the function under consideration can span the organisational structure. As already seen the function (process) of processing an order involves finance, sales and warehousing each of which will typically reside under a different part of the organization's management structure.

If the analyst is sufficiently knowledgeable of the organization's business, a global data model may be constructed first and be refined over time as information is obtained from the process analysis of the functional areas. The way data and process analysis interact is shown in Figure 26.

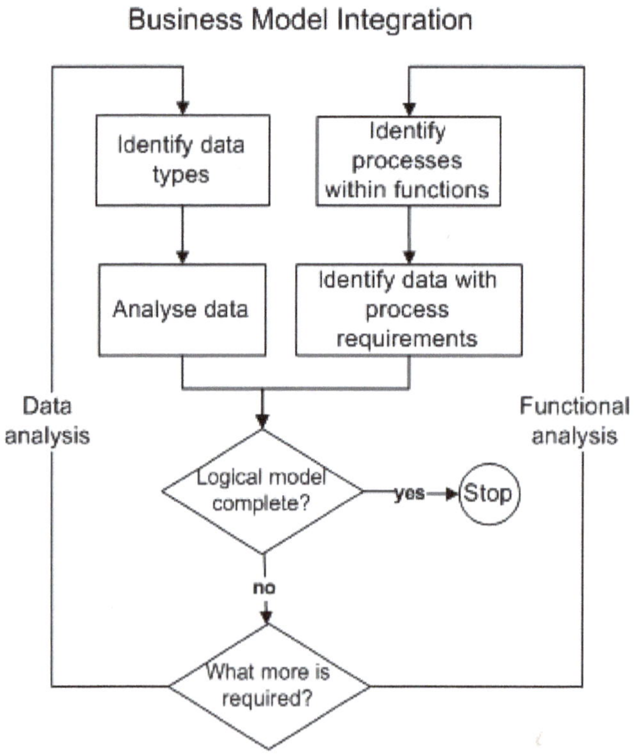

Figure 26 Interaction of data and process analysis
(Created using SSADM Professional Workbench)

OTHER MODELLING TECHNIQUES

Under this heading is grouped a vast array of approaches to modelling and mapping, some of which may be formalized to some extent while others have little or no restriction as to how they might be applied. The focus of any particular technique might be on data, information or knowledge - at which point it can be useful to elaborate on the differences between these three concepts (1).

Data: *Facts, esp. numerical facts, collected together for reference or information; a piece of information, a statistic; the quantities, characters, or symbols on which operations are performed by computers and other automatic equipment.*

Information: *Communication of the knowledge of some fact or occurrence; knowledge or facts communicated about a particular subject, event, etc.; intelligence, news.*

Knowledge: *The fact of knowing a thing, state, person, etc.; acquaintance; familiarity gained by experience; acquaintance with a fact or facts; a state of being aware or informed; awareness, consciousness*

These definitions imply a form of hierarchy comprising elements of information (data) leading to assemblies of data being communicated as information (human involvement) and thence to collections of data and information gathered by and familiar to individuals. An example of such a hierarchy is shown in Figure 27.

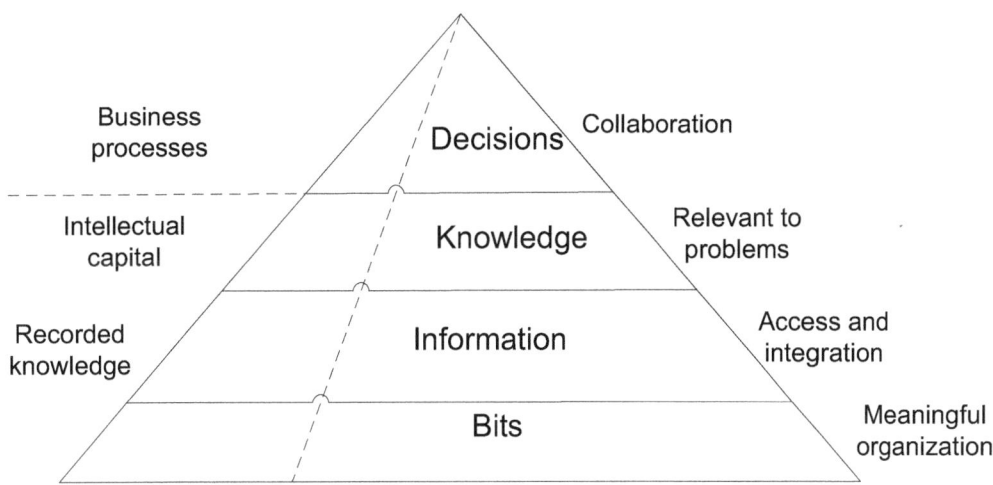

Figure 27 A Knowledge Management Hierarchy
(Created using MS Visio 2007)

From these definitions many will be able to agree on what data and information means and will acknowledge that they can reside in tangible form as electronic or physical messages or records that can be managed as 'information resources' along with other corporate resources (capital, human and so on).

'Knowledge', however, has no such tangible form. The only way it can be made a manageable information resource is for the knowledgeable person to output their experience or the facts with which they are acquainted into forms that can be recorded and reused. On this basis 'knowledge management' has no meaning; one cannot manage what an individual knows. Nevertheless, a whole industry has built itself around 'knowledge management' (KM), often simply replacing the word 'information' by 'knowledge' or rebranding products so that today's 'search engine' becomes tomorrow's 'knowledge manager'.

As far as 'Modelling' these concepts is concerned the modelling of 'data' has already been covered to some degree. 'Information modelling' is open to several interpretations and is often associated with software engineering and UML. The phrase 'Knowledge Cartography' has emerged in recent years with contrasting definitions, for example:

A process for identifying the knowledge available to an organization and mapping its location. It provides information about the location of knowledge in the organization, the person responsible for the knowledge, what the knowledge is used for, and how to access it. It serves as a map or directory to the present knowledge environment and it can illustrate knowledge gaps in the value chain (34).

The process, methods and tools for analyzing knowledge areas in order to discover features or meaning and to visualize them in a comprehensive, transparent form such that the business-relevant features are clearly highlighted (35)

and

The art, craft, science, design and engineering of different genres or map to describe intellectual landscapes and the study of cartographic practices in both beginners and experts (36).

The first two definitions relate more to mapping where knowledge resides in an organisation and who is 'in the know'. The latter approach may do the same but has a much wider compass.

The standardised methods discussed earlier come under the heading of 'visual specification languages' interpretable by software and defined as '*a set of diagrams which are valid "sentences" in that language where a diagram is a collection of "symbols" in a two or three dimensional space*' (37). Before UML and BPMN were created recourse was made to simpler flow charts and similar diagrams. These still have value now, so will be discussed next before delving into those that are mainly focused on specific application areas.

PROCESS AND DATA FLOW DIAGRAMS

Analysing and modelling processes and information inputs and outputs can be used for a number of reasons and in a variety of situations, for example to study processes and associated information as they currently exist, thereby providing a baseline for planned change or to identify opportunities for change. Possible benefits of revised or new processes and the resource implications can also be investigated, and in the case of UML or BMPN models discussed earlier, the detail necessary for programming workflow or similar systems might be provided. The models may also record sources and recipients of information

The analysis is usually undertaken functional area by functional area as each will have a reasonably coherent set of processes to examine. The analysis will reveal information flows between the functions and elsewhere thereby building a business-wide view. Data models for each area may also be created at this time.

Two main types of process model are flow charts and data flow diagrams (DFD) (The activity diagrams of UML noted in Figure 13 are essentially their object-oriented equivalent). Flow charting is one of the earliest diagramming methods used by programmers and analysts and predates the introduction of structured approaches for developing information systems. Data flow diagrams are commonly used in structured analysis and design and show the external entities (e.g. people, organizations) from where data originates, the data flows from one process to another and where the data is stored.

Clearly both types of diagram can be used to examine any process irrespective of whether computer-based solutions are being sought.

Data Flow Diagrams

A DFD for managing a sales database is shown in Figure 28 and was created using Select SSADM Professional Workbench. This tool that has been around for over 20 years and is one with which I am familiar, so I have used it here for that reason. However, I could quite easily have chosen to use Microsoft Visio - it is entirely up to the user to decide what is easiest and most suitable for the task in hand.

The various diagramming shapes will differ somewhat from one tool to another. Here they are made up of:

- Numbered rectangles: denoting processes which take information inputs, process it in some way and send the result onwards;

- Open-ended rectangles: representing information stores; those coded 'D' store data (if there was a manual store for physical information or objects it would be marked 'M');

- Ovals represent external entities (actors) which are sources of, or destinations for information (the 'Sales Staff' oval has a line through it to indicate that the icon appears more than once on the diagram);

- Arrows: denoting information flows which can be electronic (single arrow heads) or physical resources (double arrow heads), the latter not shown here.

Descriptions or notes can usually be associated with each process, store, entity or flow.

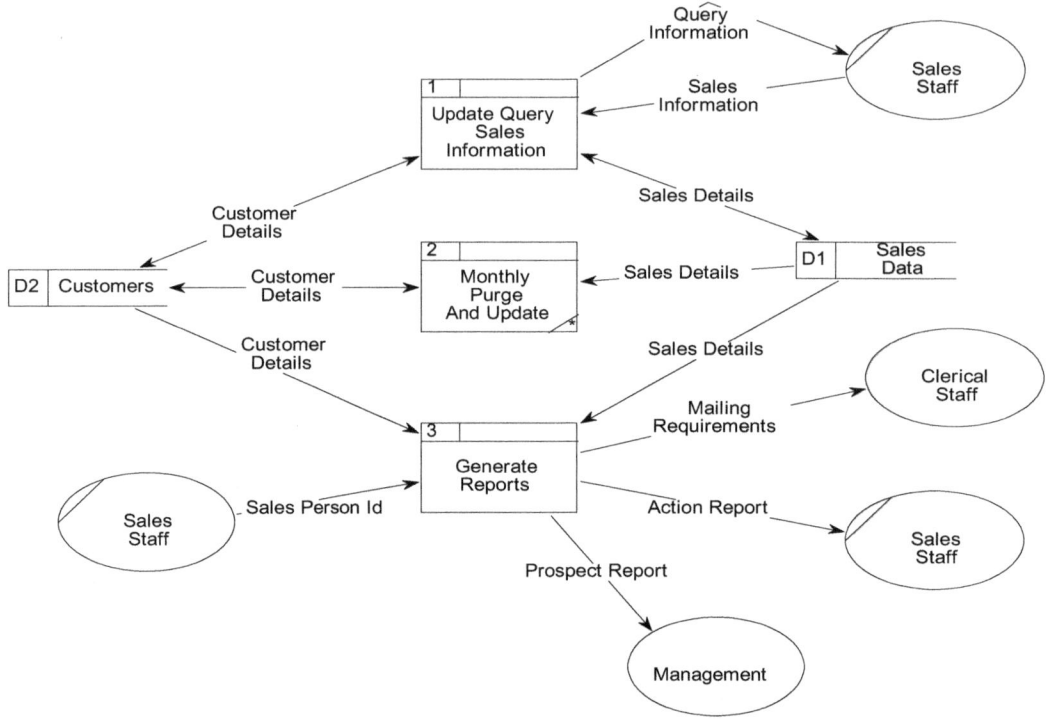

Figure 28 DFD of managing a sales database
(Created usingSelect SSADM Professional Workbench)

The diagram represents one analyst's views of how to represent the process. Another analyst may depict the processes and flows somewhat differently, but either view may provide a perfectly valid basis on which to seek improvements, 'reengineer' the processes or inform future design.

Flow charts

The data flow diagram in Figure 28 is used to produce a flow chart of the required activities as shown in Figure 29.

The drawing conventions are

- Rectangles represent activities

- Diamond shapes denote decision points

- Arrows indicate control flows

The main differences between the DFD and the flow chart are that the latter tends to be more detailed as it closely follows the logic of the business process and it depicts decision points wherever they are needed.

Although a drawing tool was used to create the DFD and flow chart, they could equally have been produced by hand which does have the advantage of immediacy.

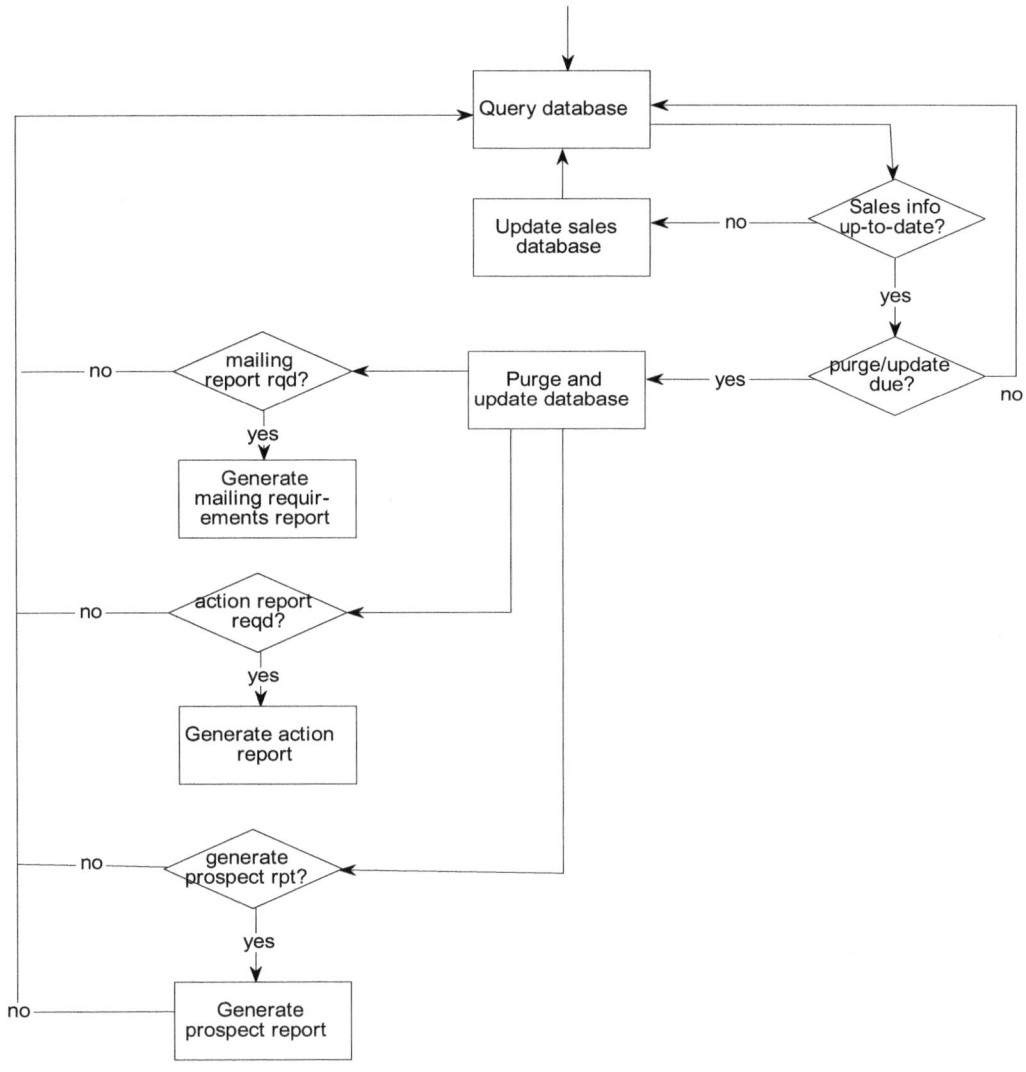

Figure 29 Flow chart of managing a sales database
(Created using Select SSADM Professional Workbench)

The choice of which type of process flow diagram to use may depend on a number of factors ranging from personal preferences to the need to conform to an employee's standard offering. Numerous articles are to be found comparing one technique with another. Johansson (37), for example, posed the question: *'which are the relevant graphical business process modelling techniques to be used when modelling a problematic and complex situation?'*

He evaluated four process modelling techniques: flowchart/nodemaps, Business Process Modelling Notation (BPMN), Event Driven Process Chains (EPC), and UML activity diagrams. All except EPC have been covered in this Viewpoint due to their wide applicability independent of any vendor. Johansson cited EPC due to its popularity within the Reference Model in SAP, which is a commercial enterprise resource planning, and hence is not dealt with here.

The four techniques were examined against the following quality principles devised by Moody (38): discriminability, perceptual and cognitive limits, emphasis, cognitive integration, perceptual directness, structure, identification, expressiveness, and simplicity.

The principles were applied to discuss the benefits and drawbacks of a specific model created with the help of a modelling technique. This is not the place to explain in more detail the meanings on the principles. Suffice to say all the techniques satisfied to some extent the seven but only BPMN reached an acceptable level.

MIND MAPPING

Mind mapping is one way to visually organize information. It typically comprises a central theme - the focus of attention - drawn in the middle of a page (or screen if software is used) to which are attached branches representing anything (topics, entities, images etc) that is logically associated with the theme. Each branch may grow linearly or add sub-branches as further thoughts are recorded - something like an octopus.

Mind mapping was popularized in the 1970s by the late Tony Buzan, an English author, educationalist and broadcaster. A 'Buzan' mind map is shown in Figure 30.

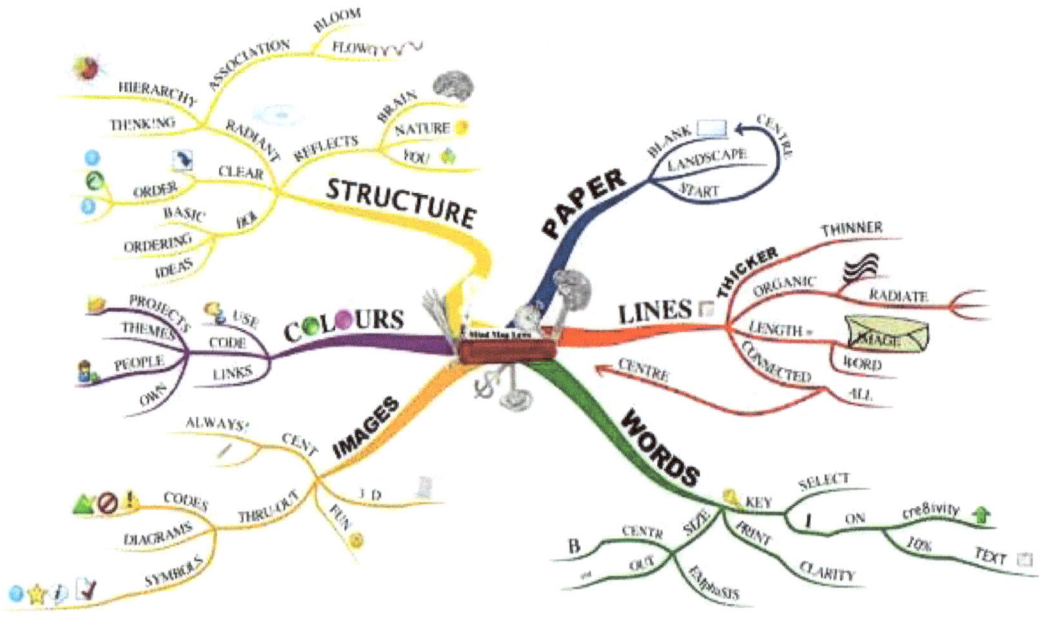

Figure 30 The make-up of a Buzan-type Mind Map
(Reproduced with permission - http://www.tonybuzan.com/about/mind-mapping/)

Buzan outlines 7 steps to making a Mind Map

1. Start in the CENTRE of a blank page turned sideways. Why? Because starting in the centre gives your Brain freedom to spread out in all directions and to express itself more freely and naturally.

2. Use an IMAGE or PICTURE for your central idea. Why? Because an image is worth a thousand words and helps you use your Imagination. A central image is more interesting, keeps you focussed, helps you concentrate, and gives your Brain more of a buzz!

3. Use COLOURS throughout. Why? Because colours are as exciting to your Brain as are images. Colour adds extra vibrancy and life to your Mind Map, adds tremendous energy to your Creative Thinking, and is fun!

4. CONNECT your MAIN BRANCHES to the central image and connect your second- and third-level branches to the first and second levels, etc. Why? Because your Brain

works by association. It likes to link two (or three, or four) things together. If you connect the branches, you will understand and remember a lot more easily.

5. Make your branches CURVED rather than straight-lined. Why? Because having nothing but straight lines is boring to your Brain.

6. Use ONE KEY WORD PER LINE. Why? Because single key words give your Mind Map more power and flexibility.

7. Use IMAGES throughout. Why? Because each image, like the central image, is also worth a thousand words. So if you have only 10 images in your Mind Map, it's already the equal of 10,000 words of notes!

Buzan developed software (iMindMap) to support his approach and trade marked the term 'Mind Map' (39). This, however, has not prevented the terms mind map, mind mapping or others being applied to a wide range of similar techniques and software (40). Hence there are 'spider diagrams' whose structures are generally not so constrained (Buzan demands the use of colour, images and keywords). A spider diagram will have a central enclosed 'bubble', and labelled sub-ideas leading off, rather than titled lines - but again this is not mandated. Spider diagrams are popular in schools being used in a variety of ways to enhance education and learning, for example note taking, researching a subject or describing a character (41).

An example of a Mind Map produced by WISE (42) to promote the breadth of opportunities and careers that women can follow in science, engineering and is shown in Figure 31.

Figure 31 A Mind Map to promote engineering as a career for women
(Reproduced with permission)

CONCEPT MAPPING

A Concept Map is a way to organize and represent knowledge in the form of a downward-branching hierarchical structure showing the relationships between concepts connected by arrows labelled with linking phrases. The technique was developed by Joseph Novak and his research team at Cornell University based on the cognitive theories of David Ausubel who stressed the importance of prior knowledge and relating new concepts to what you knew, so that meaningful deep learning can occur. The work originated in the education community where it was proving difficult to assess the understanding of elementary science students. Out of the necessity to find a better way to represent children's conceptual understanding emerged the idea of representing children's knowledge in the form of a concept map.

In contrast to mind mapping, concept mapping has richer evidence-based justification for its workings and outcomes as exemplified in papers by Novak and others (43, 44, 45).

The main elements of a concept map are shown in Figure 32 and are generally read from top to bottom, although they may appear in other forms such as a spider diagram or hierarchy.

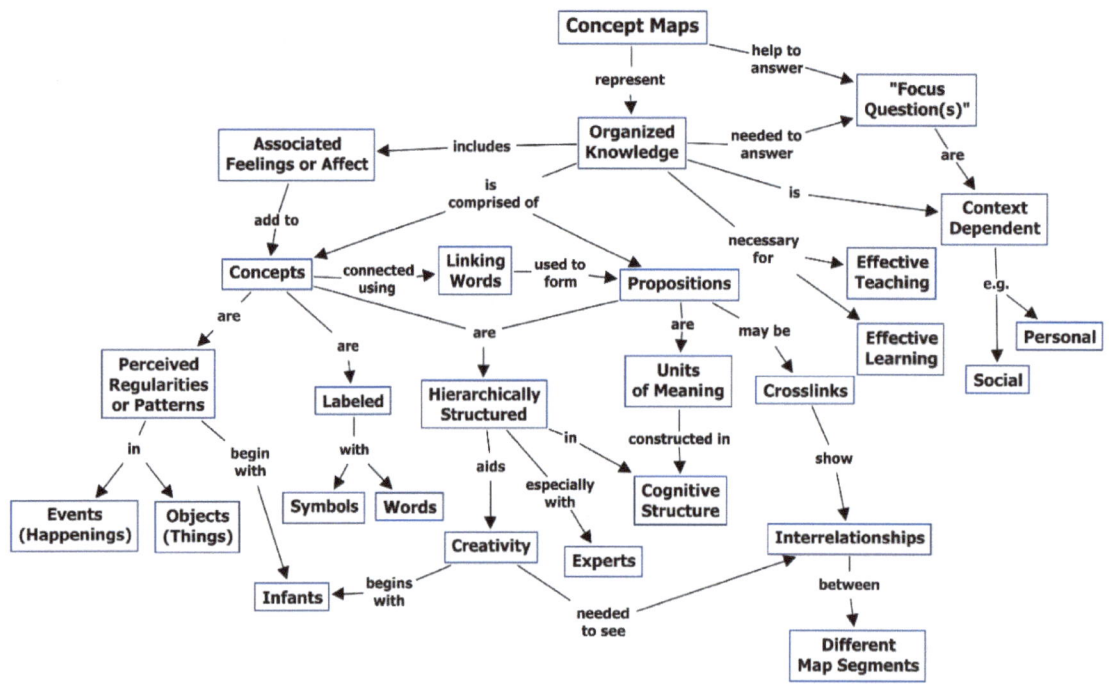

Figure 32 The key features of Concept Maps
(Reproduced with permission (43))

A well-constructed concept map will have the concepts and nodes correctly identified, the lines and arrows will correctly link concepts together into clusters or hierarchies and any propositions or statements on the lines between concepts will accurately describe how the two concepts are related.

An example of a 'fully-formed' concept map relating to photosynthesis is shown in Figure 33 (46). It presents the following statements in diagrammatic form:

1. Plants absorb water
2. Plants absorb CO2
3. Plants trap sunlight
4. Water is transported to leaves
5. CO_2 is found in the air
6. Sunlight is a source of energy
7. Ait diffuses into leaves
8. Energy drives photosynthesis
9. Photosynthesis occurs in leaves
10. Photosynthesis produces food

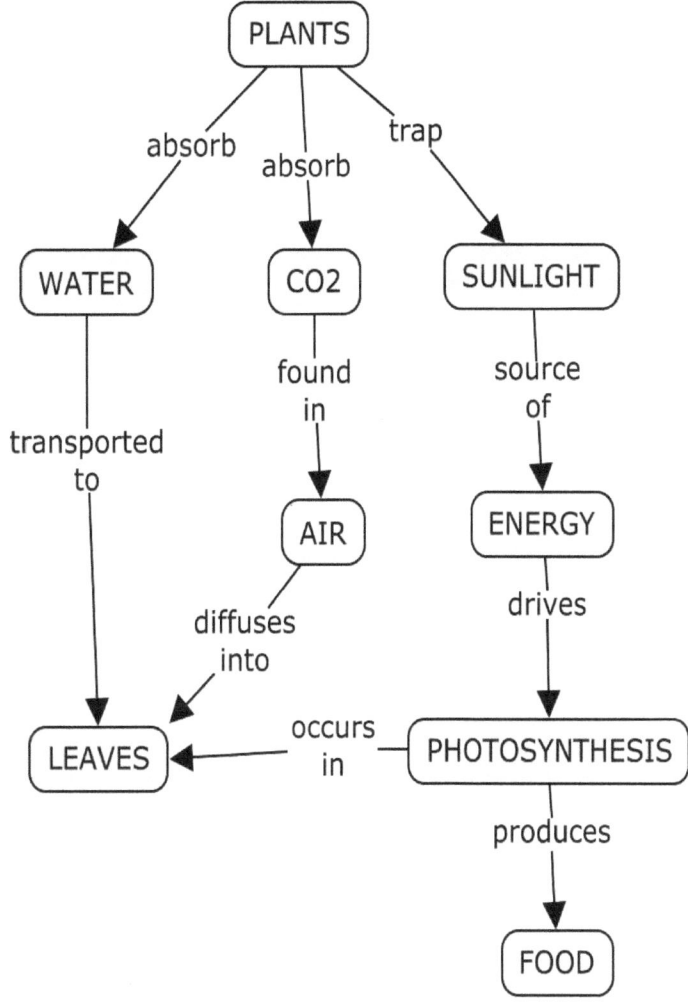

Figure 33 Concept map of plant photosynthesis (Created using Cmap Tools (http://cmap.ihmc.us/products/))

The technique has been applied in a number of fields for problem solving and mapping concepts (44) including enhancing team effectiveness, ecological management and engineering design. It can be used as the initial stage of data modelling as the diagramming conventions are likely to be more readily comprehended by non-IT staff than the UML or data models described earlier. An example of Concept Mapping to tease out the attributes relating a purchase order is shown in Figure 34.

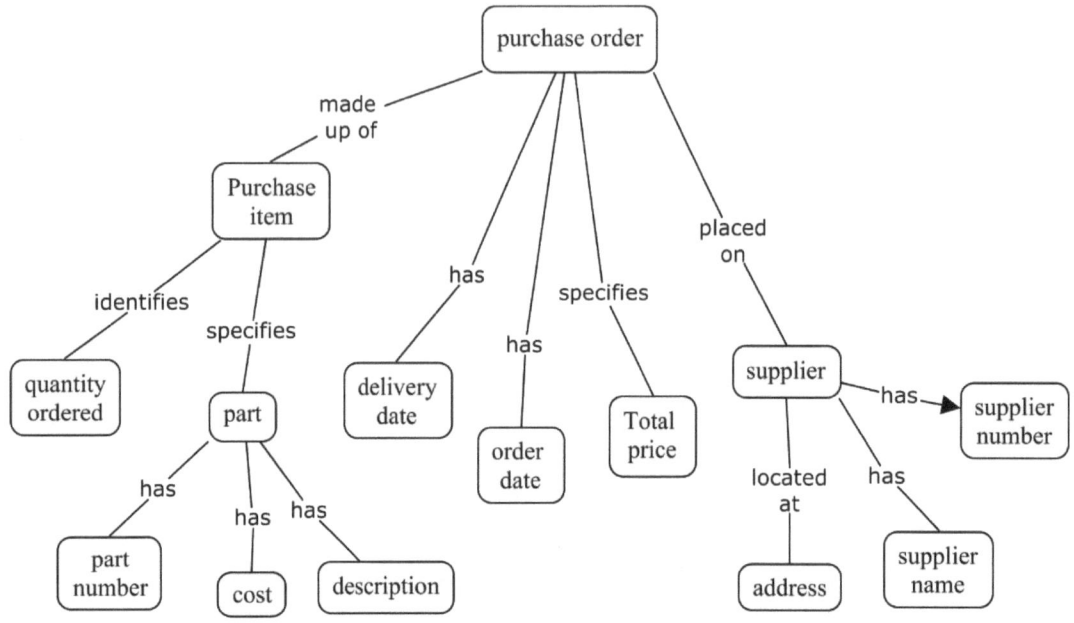

Figure 34 A concept map of a purchase order
(Created using Cmap Tools (http://cmap.ihmc.us/products/)

The product is supported by a software suite CmapTools which is available for free download. Its use not only facilitates the construction of computer-based Concept Maps but enables users to hyperlink the maps and collaborate over the internet. Biannual conferences of Concept Mappers also foster the sharing of developments and applications.

ARGUMENT AND EVIDENCE MAPPING

An argument map or diagram is a visual representation of the structure of an argument and is an aid to critical thinking. It typically includes the key components of the argument, traditionally called the conclusion and the premises, but can also show co-premises, objections, counterarguments and rebuttals (47). They are much used in the legal profession as regards examination of evidence - should this evidence be believed? If not, why not?

An argument map is like a flow chart with interconnected boxes. It is similar to other mapping activities such as mind mapping and concept mapping, but focuses on the logical, evidential or inferential relationships among propositions (48). While there are variations in detail the basic structure is shown in Figure 35.

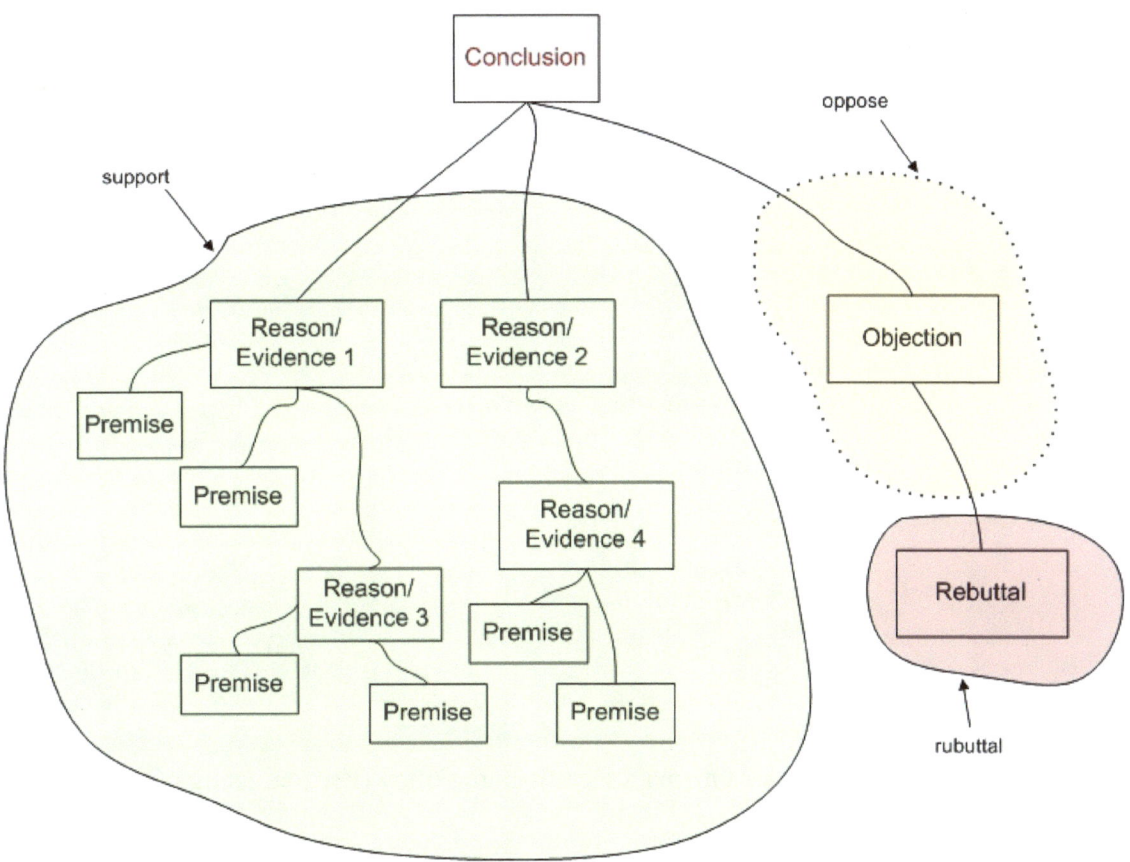

Figure 35 Structure of an argument or evidence map
(Created using MS Visio 2007)

Given the nature of the matter being addressed there are guidelines or rules for constructing an argument map. Importantly each box should contain a full sentence (not a phrase) and should be declaring something, taking a position (whether it is true or false). It should contain one and only one 'conclusion' which is the main point that an argument is attempting to prove. This conclusion is supported by 'reasons' (in the case of argument-focussed maps) or 'evidence' (for legal cases). These in turn have premises (or co-premises) each of which must be true for the reason to support the claim. There will be objections which provide evidence against the claim and possibly rebuttals which are objection to an objection (49).

An example of an argument map is provided in Figure 36 relating to President Obama's Health Policy (48). Its content conforms to the guidelines but the look differs because different software has been used. Nevertheless, the structure of the argument is made clear by the use of colours, position and icons.

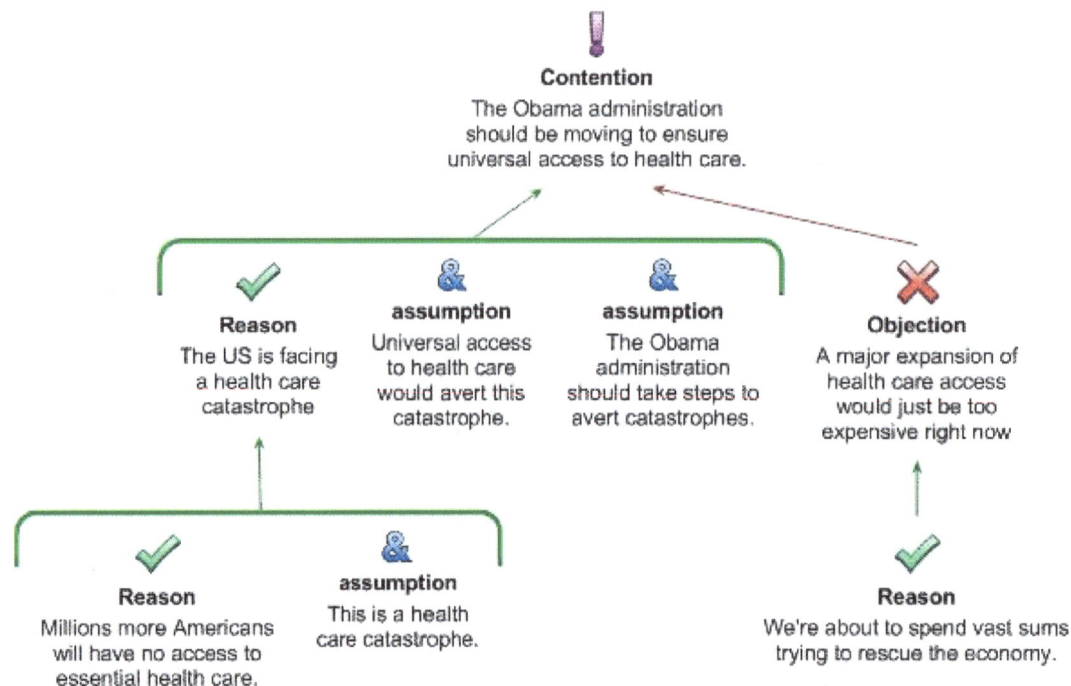

Figure 36 Argument map for Obama's Health Care policy (Created using bCisive)

Evidence Gap Mapping

A mapping technique unrelated to evidence mapping as just described is evidence gap mapping, or just evidence mapping - the latter phrasing is more common in the medical field. It is used anywhere where policymakers and practitioners wish to explore the findings and quality of the existing (mainly published) evidence on a topic, and to facilitate evidence-based decision-making (50), (51). Evidence gap maps (EGM) exists in various forms.

The International Initiative for Impact Evaluation (3ie) is an international grant-making NGO promoting evidence-informed development policies and programmes. 3ie's EGMs aim to consolidate what is known and what is not known about 'what works' in a particular sector or sub-sector by mapping out existing and ongoing systematic reviews and impact evaluations in that sector. 3ie's EGMs are interactive and have a table-like structure with interventions on the y axis and outcomes on the x axis. 'Bubble's appearing at intersections between interventions and outcomes denote the existence of a study or studies examining the relevant outcome and intervention. The larger the bubble, the greater the volume of evidence in that cell. The basic structure of the map is shown in Figure 37. In a real EGM, hovering over a bubble displays a list of all the included studies in a given cell. Bubbles of different colours indicate different types of evidence. Green (high confidence), orange (medium confidence) and red (low confidence) bubbles correspond to systematic reviews.

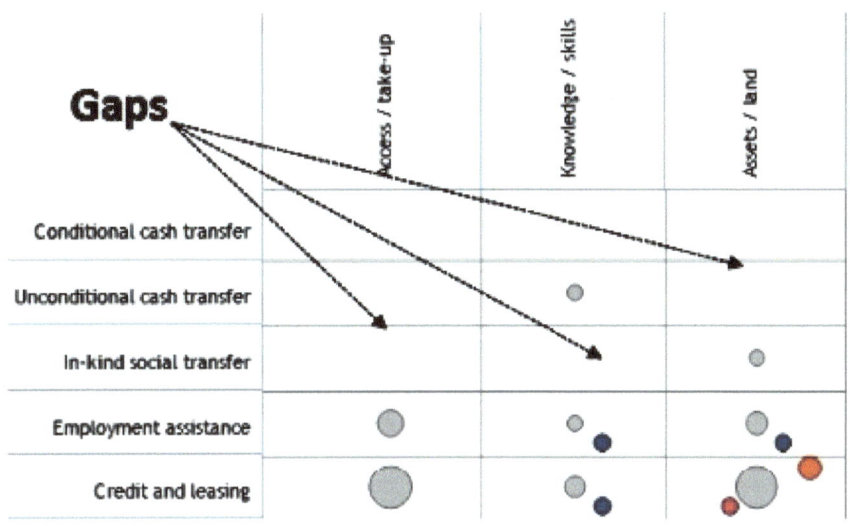

Figure 37 Structure of a 3ie Evidence Gap Map (50)
(Reproduced with permission)

A different design of evidence map is shown in Figure 38 and deals with 'mindfulness'. The practice of mindfulness, from ancient Buddhist roots, involves being aware moment-to-moment, of one's subjective conscious experience from a first-person perspective (52). Note that this work arises in the medical field and is not referred to as an evidence 'gap' map.

The bubble plot broadly summarizes mindfulness intervention systematic reviews published to February 2014 and shows the clinical conditions addressed in reviews (bubbles), the estimated size of the literature (y-axis), the effectiveness trend according to reviews (x-axis), and the number of reviews (bubble size) per clinical condition. The colours denote the type of intervention used.

ISSUE AND DIALOGUE MAPPING

Both these forms of mapping arise from the work in the late 1970s of Werner Kunz and Horst Rittel (53) on IBIS (issue-based information system), an argumentation-based approach to tackling 'wicked' problems – complex, ill-defined problems that involve multiple stakeholders (54). Note that such 'fuzzy' problems are just the ones that might be addressed using the soft systems methodology discussed earlier.

The early applications of IBIS were manually-based, but developments in technology led to the emergence of supporting products.

Issue Mapping

Issue mapping aids critical thinking by bringing together the problems, solutions, thoughts and opinions to throw light on the detailed structure and elements of an issue - defined as *'an important topic or problem for debate or discussion'* (1).

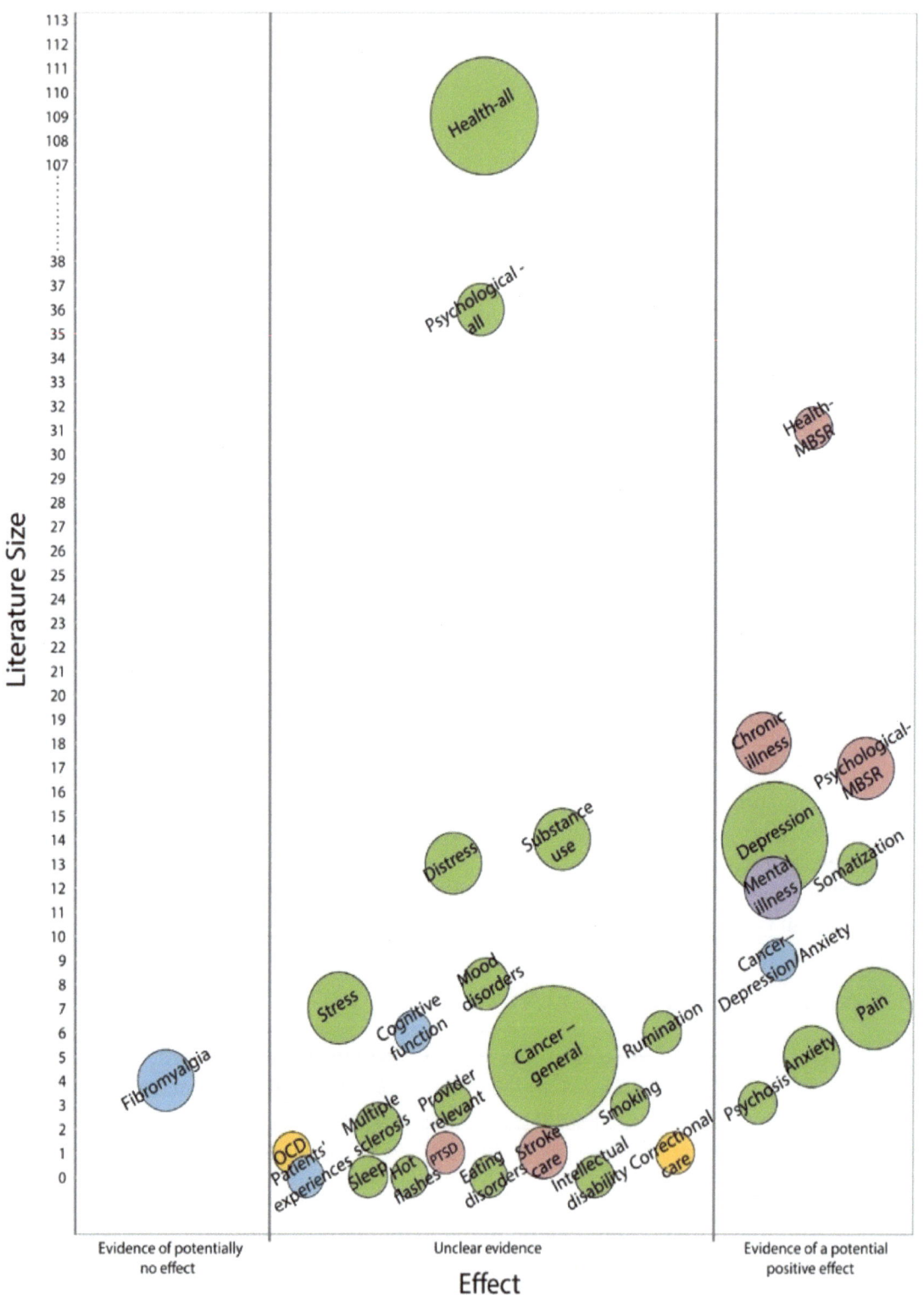

Figure 38 Evidence map of mindfulness (52)
(Creation tool not identified)

The use of IBIS relies on posing questions of which there are seven key types (55):

1. Deontic: What should we do?
2. Instrumental: How should we do X?5
3. Criterial: What are the criteria for success?
4. Factual: What is X?
5. Conceptual: What does X mean?
6. Explanatory: Why is X?
7. Contextual: What is the background?

These can be distilled into four basic elements - Question, Idea (or Answer), Pro arguments and Con arguments, assembled according to a basic grammatical structure that builds the 'map' of the issues under discussion. The resultant map is read form left to right – See Figure 39 (56).

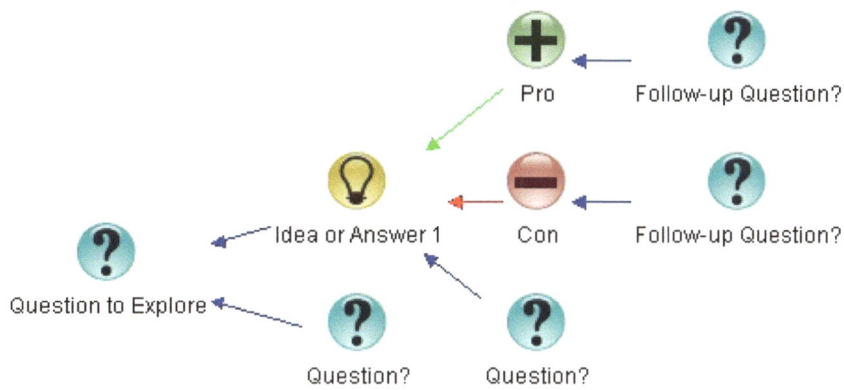

Figure 39 Basic structure of an issue map (56)
(Created using Compendium)

An example issue map relating to a budget issue is shown in Figure 40 (57).

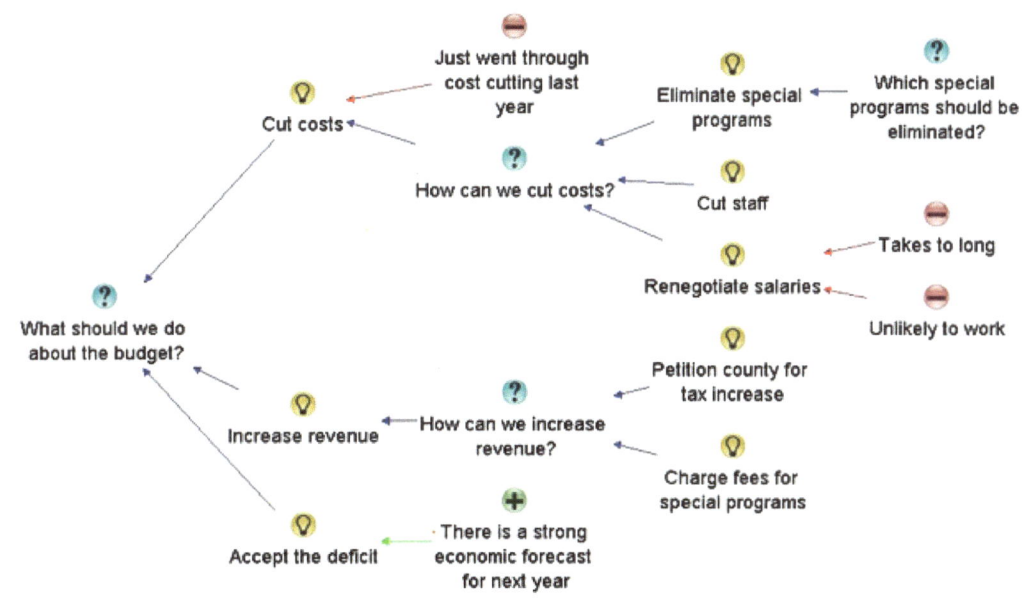

Figure 40 Issue map to address a budget problem (57)
(Created using Compendium)

Dialogue mapping

Dialogue mapping came later and has been described as issue mapping with group facilitation (55). It involves a facilitator trained in the technique, a means to display the progress and outcome of the discussion and the use of IBIS as the grammatical language. The development of the technique originated with Jeff Conklin and his Cognexus Institute (58).

Although the use of the Compendium tool is closely associated with issue and dialogue mapping, alternatives can be deployed. Figure 41 shows a discussion map created using a mind mapping product, MindManager (59).

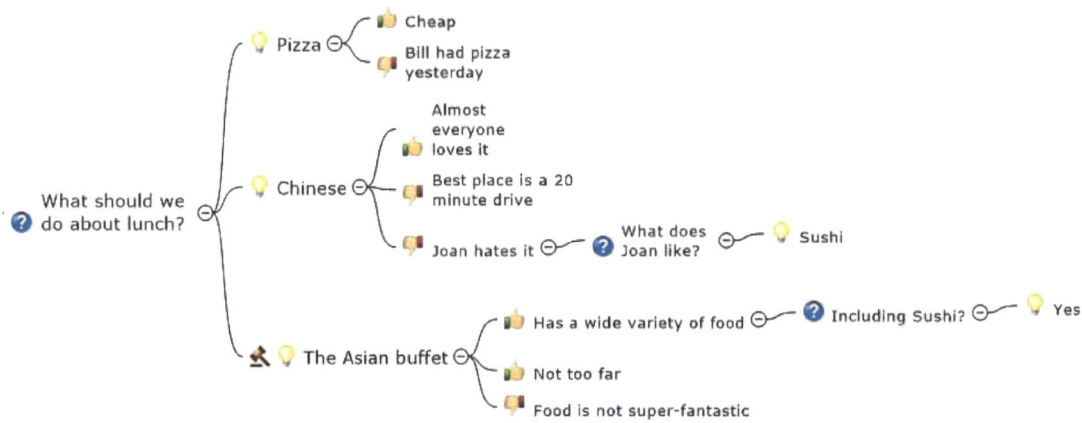

Figure 41 A dialogue map produced using MindManager (59)

SKETCHNOTES

Moving somewhat away from the preceding more structured techniques there are Sketchnotes. These are hand drawn visual records of ideas, or are made while listening to a speaker or reading a book. Their use has been promulgated in the class rooms (60) and to a wider audience (61), with research showing the benefit of drawing as note-taking (62). Increasingly use is being made of tablets and associated software to 'doodle' and create sketchnotes (63).

An example of a Sketchnote is provided in Figure 42 depicting the main points from a talk concerning problems relating to education (64). The Sketchnote depicts various stakeholders (pupils, teachers and by implication the US government) and records some of the tensions and problems within education in the United States. In this regard it is akin to a Rich Picture within a soft systems study as discussed earlier.

Figure 42 Sketchnote of 'How-To-Escape-Educations-Death-Valley'

MODELLING TOOLS – A CAVEAT

The focus of this Viewpoint is on techniques rather than the supporting modelling tools. This is deliberate as the thinking behind the modelling process is more important than the technology deployed in making the outcome visible. Inevitably examples of commercially available modelling software are cited throughout the Viewpoint, but that should not necessarily be taken as an endorsement of their suitability. The modelling tools market is large and fluctuating with new players emerging and existing ones either falling out of favour or becoming redundant as they are unable to work on updated or new operating systems. Intending users need to do their own research to find the most appropriate tool. It may well be that those with which they are already familiar will prove to be perfectly adequate. On the other hand, decisions on, for example, the need to collaborate with others might sway the choice made.

RESOURCES LIST

The resource listing mirrors those in the content headings

The Systems Movement

Flood, R.L. and Carson, E.R. (1988) *Dealing with complexity*. London. Plenum Press. (An introduction to the theory and application of system science).

The International Society for the Systems Sciences [Online: http://isss.org/world/about-the-isss]. [Accessed 22 February 2016]

Universal Modelling Language

Ambler, S.W., (2004) *The Object Primer. Agile model-driven development with UML 2.0..* Cambridge University Press.

Fowler, M. (2004) *UML Distilled. A brief guide to the standard object modelling language'*. Pearson Education, Boston

Data Modelling

Ready-made data models for Enterprise Data Models, over 1400 in 50 categories [Online: http://www.databaseanswers.org/data_models/index.htm]. [Accessed 22 February 2016]

Silverston. L. *The Data Model Resource Books*. Series of books providing universal data models for all enterprises. the models (figures) can be downloaded from the publisher. [Online: http://eu.wiley.com/WileyCDA/Section/id-WILEYEUROPE2_SEARCH_RESULT.html?query=len%20silverston]. [Accessed 22 February 2016]

Process modelling

Gartner. *Magic quadrant for intelligent business process management suites*. 18 March 2015. [Online: https://www.gartner.com/doc/3009617/magic-quadrant-intelligent-business-process]. [Accessed 25 February 2016]

Business Process Model and Notation

Sherry, K.J. (2015) *Complete BPMN Pocket Reference; a Comprehensive Reference Guide to BPMN including Specification version* 2.0.2. Admaks Publishing

Comparison of Business Process Modelling Notation tools [Online: https://en.wikipedia.org/wiki/Comparison_of_Business_Process_Modeling_Notation_tools]. [Accessed 22 February 2016]:

BPMN 2.0 Business Process Model and Notation Poster. [Online: http://www.bpmb.de/index.php/BPMNPoster]. [Accessed 25 February 2016]

Mind Mapping

Buzan, T. and Griffiths, C. (2014) *Mind Maps for Business*. 2nd edition London Pearson

Software for mind mapping and information organisation [Online: http://www.mind-mapping.org/]. [Accessed 22 February 2016]

50 useful mind maps for students (sourced from associatedegree.org) [Online: http://www.associatesdegree.com/2009/07/27/50-useful-mind-mapping-tools-for-college-students/]. [Accessed 26 April 2019]

Concept Mapping

Cognitive approach to learning. Ausubel's Assimilation Theory. [Online: https://sites.google.com/site/cognitiveapproachtolearning/ausubel-s-assimilation-theory]

Concept map assessments. Centre for Enhancement of Teaching and Learning. [Online: http://ar.cetl.hku.hk/am_cm.htm]. [Accessed 22 February 2016]

Moon, Brian M. et al, (2011) *Applied Concept Mapping: Capturing, Analyzing, and Organizing Knowledge,* Boca Raton. CRC Press

Raubenheimer, D. and Oliver, K. *Alternative Assessment with Electronic Concept Mapping Software* [Online: https://www.learntechlib.org/p/22013/]. [Accessed 31 July 2017] (Provides guidance on producing concept maps and of assessing how well they are constructed; also identifies mapping tools).

Concept Mapping in the Classroom [Online: http://www.schrockguide.net/concept-mapping.html]. [Accessed 22 February 2016] (Comprehensive guide to producing and creating concept maps).

Argument and Evidence Mapping

What is argument mapping? [Online: https://www.reasoninglab.com/argument-mapping/]. [Accessed 26 April 2019]

What is Argument Mapping? (Step-by-step introduction) [Online: https://ethicalrealism.wordpress.com/2012/12/31/what-is-argument-mapping/]. [Accessed 22 February 2016]

Critical thinking on the web (lists of sources and tools). [Online: http://www.austhink.com/critical/pages/argument_mapping.html]. [Accessed 23 February 2016]

A new beginning: introducing argdown. [Online: http://www.argunet.org/]. [Accessed 26 April 2019]

Argument diagramming tools (list of software) [Online: http://www.phil.cmu.edu/projects/argument_mapping/]. [Accessed 25 February 2016]

Evidence gap maps

Evidence gap maps - a tool for promoting evidence-informed policy and prioritizing future research. (provides an introduction to evidence-gap maps, outlines the gap-map methodology, and presents some examples) [Online: http://documents.worldbank.org/curated/en/2013/12/18648542/evidence-gap-maps-tool-promoting-evidence-informed-policy-prioritizing-future-research]. [Accessed 25 February 2016]

Issue and Dialogue Mapping

Issue Mapping Online. (offers a set of digital techniques for the detection, analysis and visualisation of topical affairs). [Online: http://www.issuemapping.net/Main/WebHome]. [Accessed 25 February 2016]

A Tool for Wicked Problems: Dialogue Mapping FAQs. [Online: http://www.cognexus.org/id41.htm]. [Accessed 25

Rearchitecting a Software Platform. A Beginner's Case Study with Dialog Mapping. [Online: http://eekim.com/papers/2002/acmht/index.html]. [Accessed 25 February 2016]

Sketchnotes

Neill, D. An educators guide to sketchnoting. [Online: http://www.thegraphicrecorder.com/an-educators-guide-to-sketchnoting/]. [Accessed 25 February 2016]

OTHER RESOURCES

International Forum of Visual Practitioners. [Online: https://www.ifvp.org/]. [Accessed 26 April 2019]

Visual literacy (This e-learning site focuses on a critical, but often neglected skill for business, communication, and engineering students, namely visual literacy, or the ability to evaluate, apply, or create conceptual visual representations) [Online: http://www.visual-literacy.org/index.html]. [Accessed 25 February 2016]

Okada, A., Buckingham Shum, S.J. and Sherbourne, T. (Eds). *Knowledge Cartography.* London. 2014 Springer (already noted as reference 36. The 22 chapters from researchers and practitioners covering numerous techniques and associated software including mind, concept, argument, dialogue and evidence mapping.

Spiegelhalter, D. (2019) *The Art of Statistics*. Penguin Random House UK (Includes ways to represent and display statistics in visual form

ANNEX A DATA NORMALIZATION

The process of data normalization in relation to the purchase order in Figure 20 is explained in this Annex.

The details about the purchase order (the entity being considered - or 'object in UML terms) can be written as follows to describe its make-up which is uniquely identified by the Order Number and is underlined:

Purchase Order (Order Number, Supplier Number, Supplier Name, Supplier Address, Order Date, Delivery Date, (Part Number, Part Description, Quantity Ordered, Line Item Price), Total Price)

However, some of the information (the attributes) is difficult to obtain. For example, to find the total quantity ordered of a particular part one would have to go through every purchase order to find each occurrence of the part number.

On examining the entity, the group (Part Number, Part Description, Quantity Ordered, Line Item Price) is seen to be a repeating group as several of these Purchase Items make up an order. So if it is separated out as a new entity type, **Purchase Item** it would be easier to access individual purchase items. This produces the following two entities and represents the first step in normalization (indicated by the suffix '-1'), to remove repeating groups and rewrite them as new entities.

PurchaseOrder-1 (Order Number, Supplier Number, Supplier Name, Supplier Address, Order Date, Delivery Date, Total Price)

PurchaseItem-1 (Order Number, Part Number, Part Description, Quantity Ordered, Line Item Price)

The attribute Order Number is required in the **Purchase Item-1** entity to retain the original information that a purchase item is related to a particular purchase order. Order Number and Part Number are composite identifiers for the entity **Purchase Item-1,** i.e. both identifiers are required to uniquely identify a purchase item.

Examining the **Purchase Item-1** entity shows that the attribute Part Description is not functionally dependent on the whole of the identifier for the entity as it relates only to the Part. Hence it should be separated out as another entity as a second step in normalization.

PurchaseOrder-2 (Order Number, Supplier Number, Supplier Name, Supplier Address, Order Date, Delivery Date, Total Price)

PurchaseItem-2 (Order Number, Part Number, Quantity Ordered, Line Item Price)

Part-2 (Part Number, Part Description)

This avoids repetition of part descriptions in purchase items. It also enables details of parts and additions of new parts to be managed independently of whether they are part of an order.

Further examination of the purchase order entity **Purchase Order-2** shows that there is functional dependency between the non-identifying attributes Supplier Number, Supplier

Name and Supplier Address. Hence further rationalisation is possible by separating these out as the third step of normalization to arrive at the following entities.

PurchaseOrder-3 (Order Number, Supplier Number, Order Date, Delivery Date, Total Price)

PurchaseItem-3 (Order Number, Part Number, Quantity Ordered, Line Item Price)

Part-3 (Part Number, Part Description)

Supplier-3 (Supplier Number, Supplier Name, Supplier Address)

These four entities form the logical data model in Figure 21.

LIST OF FIGURES

Concept map of the Viewpoint's content

Figure 1 Shannon and Wear Communication Model

Figure 2 The Systems Praxis Framework

Figure 3 The Systems Movement

Figure 4 System boundaries of Engineered, Social and Natural systems

Figure 5 Stripy patterns produced by electrons passing through a pair of slits

Figure 6a A ladder deck bridge at construction stage

Figure 6b Grillage model for a ladder deck bridge

Figure 6c Ladder deck 3D model for interaction of cross-girders and main girders

Figure 7 Simplified modelling of three plausible interconnected scenarios for the Galapagos social-ecological system, showing the tourism model as the main indirect driver of change

Figure 8 Generalised systems analysis processes

Figure 9 The SIMILAR tasks for Systems Engineering

Figure 10 Examples of operations research techniques

Figure 11 Stages of the soft systems methodology

Figure 12 Comparison of hard and soft methodologies

Figure 13 UML Diagram Types

Figure 14 What people think of UML

Figure 15 UML/BPMN usage in general

Figure 16 Class model for a customer order

Figure 17 Sequence model for a customer order

Figure 18 Structured and unstructured information

Figure 19 Types of data model

Figure 20 Purchase order example

Figure 21 Entity relationship diagram of the purchase order

Figure 22 A BPMN diagram of an order process

Figure 23 Types of graphical notations used in BPMN

Figure 24 Use case text for process an order

Figure 25 Use case diagram for process an order

Figure 26 Interaction of data and process analysis

Figure 27 A Knowledge Management Hierarchy

Figure 28 DFD of managing a sales database

Figure 29 Flow chart of managing a sales database

Figure 30 The make-up of a Buzan-type Mind Map

Figure 31 A mind map to promote engineering as a career for women

Figure 32 The key features of Concept Map

Figure 33 Concept map of plant photosynthesis

Figure 34 A concept map of a purchase order

Figure 35 Structure of an argument or evidence map

Figure 36 An argument map relating to President Obama's Health Care policy

Figure 37 Structure of a 3ie Evidence Gap Map

Figure 38 Evidence map of mindfulness

Figure 39 Basic structure of an issue map

Figure 40 Issue map to address a budget problem

Figure 41 A dialogue map produce using MindManager

Figure 42 Sketchnote of 'How-To-Escape-Educations-Death-Valley'

REFERENCES

(1) Shorter Oxford English Dictionary, 6th edition (2007) Oxford, Oxford University Press.

(2) Shannon–Weaver model. [Online: https://en.wikipedia.org/wiki/Shannon%E2%80%93Weaver_model]. [Accessed 20 August 2015]

(3) Adler, R. & Towne, N. (1978). *Looking out/looking in*. New York: Holt, Rinehart and Winston.

(4) IACACT. *Model off Communication*. [Online: http://www.iacact.com/?q=models]. [Accessed 22 November 2015]

(5) Ludwig von Bertalanffy. [Online: https://en.wikipedia.org/wiki/Ludwig_von_Bertalanffy]. [Accessed 23 August 2015]

(6) ISO/IEC/IEEE 15288:2015 *Systems and software engineering - System life cycle processes*. International Standards Organisation

(7) Singer, J., Sillitto, H., Bendz, J., Chroust, G., Hybertson, D., Lawson, H., Martin, J., Martin, R., Singer, M. & Takaku, T. (2012), *The Systems Praxis Framework, in 'Systems and Science at Crossroads – Sixteenth IFSR Conversation'*, SEA-SR-32, Inst. f. Systems Engineering and Automation, Johannes Kepler University, Linz, Austria, pp. 89–90 [Online: http://systemspraxis.org/downloads/SPFBrochureView.php]. [Accessed 24 August 2015]

(8) System Engineering Book of Knowledge Glossary. [Online: http://sebokwiki.org/wiki/Category:Glossary_of_Terms]. [Accessed 21 November 2015]

(9) Thayer, F. *General System(s) Theory: The Promise That Could Not Be Kept*. The Academy of Management Journal. 15, (4) General Systems Theory (Dec., 1972), pp. 481-493

(10) Hale, C.L. (1979). *General systems theory and organizational communication: A constructivist-coorientational perspective*. Paper presented at the Annual Meeting of the International Communication Association, Chicago. April 25-29, 1978. [Online: http://eric.ed.gov/?id=ED155756]. [Accessed 27 August 2015]

(11) Hoos, I.R., (1983). *Systems analysis in public policy - A critique*. London. University of California Press.

(12) Leighninger, Robert D. Jr. *Systems Theory*, The Journal of Sociology & Social Welfare. 2014, 5 (4), Article 2. [Online: http://scholarworks.wmich.edu/cgi/viewcontent.cgi?article=1294&context=jssw]. [Accessed 26 August 2015]

(13) Cox, B. & Forshaw, F. (2012). *The Quantum Universe: Everything that can happen does happen*. London: Penguin Books

(14) Davisson, C.J., & Germer. L.H. *Diffraction of Electrons by a Crystal of Nickel.* Physical Review 30, (6), (Dec 1927). [Online: http://journals.aps.org/pr/pdf/10.1103/PhysRev.30.705]. [Accessed 25 November 2015]

(15) Modelling and Analysis of Beam Bridges. [Online: http://www.steelconstruction.info/Modelling_and_analysis_of_beam_bridges#Modelling_options_for_a_typical_multi-beam_bridge]. [Accessed 21 November 2015]

(16) González, J. A., Montes, C., Rodríguez J., and Tapia W. (2008) *Rethinking the Galapagos Islands as a complex social-ecological system: implications for conservation and management.* Ecology and Society 13 (2): 13. [Online: http://www.ecologyandsociety.org/vol13/iss2/art13/]. [Accessed 4 August 2015]

(17) Checkland, P.B. (1981) *Systems Thinking, Systems Practice*, New York. Wiley.

(18) ISO/IEC/IEEE 24765:2010 Systems and software engineering - Vocabulary

(19) Checkland, P.B. (1978) *The Origins and Nature of 'hard' systems thinking.* Journal of Applied Systems Analysis. Vol.5.

(20) Digby, J. *Operations Research and Systems Analysis at RAND, 1948-1967.* [Online: http://www.rand.org/content/dam/rand/pubs/notes/2007/N2936.pdf]. [Accessed 25 November 2015]

(21) What is operations research? Institute for Operations Research and the Management Sciences [Online: https://www.informs.org/About-INFORMS/What-is-Operations-Research]. [Accessed 26 November 2015]

(22) OR Methods? [Online: https://www.theorsociety.com/Pages/Careers/WhatIsOR.aspx]. [Accessed 26 November 2015]

(23) Pidd, M., Brown and J., Cooper, C. *A taxing problem: The complementary use of hard and soft OR in the public sector.* Lancaster University Management School Working Paper 2003/058 19 Sept 2003. [Online: http://eprints.lancs.ac.uk/48664/1/Document.pdf]. [Accessed 28 November 2015]

(24) Object Management Group [Online: http://www.omg.org/gettingstarted/gettingstartedindex.htm]. [Accessed 1 December 2015

(25) Object Management Group [Online: https://www.omg.org/spec/UML/2.5.1/PDF], [Accessed 24 April 2019]

(26) Fowler. M. (2004) *UML Distilled,* Boston. Pearson Education

(27) Ambler, S. *Modelling and Documentation 2013 Mini-Survey Results.* [Accessed 4 January 2016] [Online: http://www.ambysoft.com/surveys/modelingDocumentation2013.html]. [Accessed 4 January 2016]

(28) Ambler, S. *UML 2.5: Do you even care?* [Online: http://www.drdobbs.com/architecture-and-design/uml-25-do-you-even-care/240163702]. [Accessed 4 January 2016]

(29) Ambler, S. *UML Data Modelling Profile* [Online: Agile Data]. [Accessed 19 January 2016]

(30) Standard data model. [Online: https://en.wikipedia.org/wiki/Standard_data_model]. [Accessed 20 January 2016]

(31) Object Management Group [https://www.omg.org/spec/BPMN/2.0.2/PDF] Business Process Model and Notation (BPMN) Version 2.0.2 [Accessed 24 April 2019]

(32) Börger, E. *Approaches to modelling business processes: a critical analysis of BPMN, workflow patterns and YAWL* Software & Systems Modelling 11, (3) pp305-318 (2012) [Online: http://www.di.unipi.it/~boerger/Papers/Bpmn/EvalBpm.pdf]. [Accessed 23 January 2015]

(33) Wohed, P. et al *On the Suitability of BPMN for Business Process Modelling* In 'Business Process Management' 4th International Conference, BPM 2006, Vienna, Austria, September 5-7, 2006. Proceedings. [Online http://www.workflowpatterns.com/documentation/documents/BPMN-eval-BPM06.pdf]. [Accessed 23 January 2016]

(34) Davenport 1997 [Online http://www.igi-global.com/dictionary/knowledge-cartography-or-mapping/16280] [Accessed 23 January 2016]

(35) Speel, P.H., Shadbolt N., De Vries W., Van Dam P.H, and O'hara K. (1999) *Knowledge Mapping for industrial purpose*. October 99, Banff, Canada. Conférence KAW99

(36) Okada, A., Buckingham Shum, S.J. and Sherbourne, T. (Eds). (2014) *Knowledge Cartography*. London. Springer.

(37) Johansson, L-O., Wärja, M. 2 and Carlsson, S, *An evaluation of business process model techniques, using Moody's quality criterion for a good diagram*. [Online: http://ceur-ws.org/Vol-963/paper5.pdf]. [Accessed 12 February 2016]

(38) Moody, D., *What makes a good diagram? improving the cognitive effectiveness of diagrams in is development*. Advances in Information Systems Development, Volume 2, Springer. 2007: p. 481-492

(39) Mind mapping Trade mark. [Online: https://www.ipo.gov.uk/tmcase/Results/1/UK00001424476?legacySearch=False /]. [Accessed 24 April 2019]

(40) Mind map. [Online: https://en.wikipedia.org/wiki/Mind_map]. [Accessed 24 April 2019]

(41) What is a spider diagram? [Online: http://www.theschoolrun.com/spider-diagrams]. [Accessed 13 February 2016]

(42) Engineering and you [Online: https://www.wisecampaign.org.uk/what-we-do/wise-projects/engineering-and-you/]. [Accessed 24 April 2019]

(43) Novak, J. D. and A. J. Cañas, *The theory underlying concept maps and how to Construct and use them*. [Online: http://cmap.ihmc.us/docs/theory-of-concept-maps]. [Accessed 20 January 2016]

(44) Safayeni, F. and Cañas, A.J.. *Concept maps: A theoretical note on concepts and the need for cyclic concept ,maps*, [Online: https://onlinelibrary.wiley.com/doi/abs/10.1002/tea.20074]. [Accessed 24 April 2019]

(45) Cañas, A.J and Novak, J. D. *Re-examining the foundations for effective use of concept maps*. [Online: http://cmc.ihmc.us/cmc2006Papers/cmc2006-p247.pdf]. [Accessed 14 February 2016]

(46) Concept map of plant photosynthesis. [Online: https://www.flickr.com/photos/lauradahl/1209849885/in/photostream/]. [Accessed 17 February 2016]

(47) Argument maps. [Online: https://en.wikipedia.org/wiki/Argument_map]. [Accessed 17 February 2016]

(48) Van Gelder, T., *What is argument mapping?* [Online: http://timvangelder.com/2009/02/17/what-is-argument-mapping/]. [Accessed 17 February 2016]

(49) Argument mapping - the basics. [Online: http://www.jostwald.com/ArgumentMapping/ARGUMENT%20MAPPING.pdf]. [Accessed 24 April 2019]

(50) How to use evidence gap maps. International Initiative for Impact Evaluation [Online: http://www.3ieimpact.org/evidence-hub/evidence-gap-maps]. [Accessed 24 April 2019]

(51) Bragge, P. et al.. *The Global Evidence Mapping Initiative: Scoping research in broad topic areas*. BMC Medical Research Methodology.2011, [Online: https://bmcmedresmethodol.biomedcentral.com/articles/10.1186/1471-2288-11-92]. [Accessed 24 April 2019]

(52) Hempel, S, Taylor, S.L, Marshall, NJ, Miake-Lye, I.M, Beroes, J M, Shanman, R, Solloway, M.R, Shekelle, P.G. *Evidence map of mindfulness*. Department of Veterans Affairs VA-ESP Project #05-226; 2014. [Online: https://www.beckley.va.gov/wholehealth/Evidence_Mindfulness.pdf]. [Accessed 25 April 2019]

(53) Kunz., W.* and Rittel, H.W. J. *Issues as elements of information system*. July 1970 (reprinted May 1979). [Online: http://citeseerx.ist.psu.edu/viewdoc/download?doi=10.1.1.134.1741&rep=rep1&type=pdf]. [Accessed 25 April 2019]

(54) Issue-based information system (IBIS). [Online: https://en.wikipedia.org/wiki/Issue-Based_Information_System]. [Accessed 20 February 2016]

(55) Issue mapping. Cognexus Institute [Online: http://www.cognexus.org/issue_mapping_faqs.htm]. [Accessed 20 February 2016]

(56) Seybold, P.B. *How to address 'wicked problems'*. 23 May 2013 [Online: http://www.customers.com/media/docs/articles/Using-Dialogue_Mapping-to-Address-Wicked-Problems-05-23-2013.pdf]. [Accessed 25 April 2019]

(57) Issue mapping webinar courses. Cognexus Institute [Online: http://www.cognexus.org/issue_mapping_webinar_series.htm]. [Accessed 26 April 2019]

(58) A Tool for Wicked Problems: Dialogue Mapping. [Online: http://www.cognexus.org/id41.htm]. [Accessed 21 February 2016]

(59) MindManager. [Online: https://www.mindjet.com/mindmanager/]. [Accessed 26 April 2019]

(60) Schrok, K. *Sketchnoting in the classroom*. [Online: http://www.schrockguide.net/sketchnoting.html]. [Accessed 21 February 2016]

(61) Sketchnotes. [Online: http://rohdesign.com/about/]. [Accessed 21 February 2016]

(62) Schwartz, K., *Taking Notes: Is The Pen Still Mightier Than the Keyboard?* [Online: http://ww2.kqed.org/mindshift/2015/08/18/taking-notes-is-the-pen-still-mightier-than-the-keyboard/]

(63) Glader, P. *These Gorgeous iPad Notes Could Lead to the Paperless Classroom*. The Journal 13 November 2013. [Online: https://thejournal.com/Articles/2013/11/13/These-Gorgeous-iPad-Notes-Could-Lead-to-the-Paperless-Classroom.aspx?Page=1]. [Accessed 21 February 2016]

(64) Sketchnotes of Ken Robinson On how to escape education's Death Valley. [Online: http://www.thegraphicrecorder.com/2014/05/21/sketchnotes-of-ken-robinson-on-how-to-escape-educations-death-valley/]. [Accessed 21 February 2016]

AUTHOR INFORMATION

Bob Wiggins consulted on a variety of information projects and ran his own company for over 20 years prior to which he established information services for the British Gas Engineering Research Station in the transition to natural gas. At BP he established and coordinated the Group's central information services, managed the data and records management consultancy teams, and introduced one of the first major corporate text retrieval systems. He was for some time Assistant Editor for the International Journal of Information Management published by Elsevier.

The first Cura Viewpoint 'Information Governance – beyond ISI 30301' was published in 2014 in electronic form.

The third edition of his book 'Effective Document and Data Management' is available: as a hardback (ISBN 9781409423287, paperback (ISBN 9781138269460) and in e-book form (ISBN 9781315578910). Some reviews:

'That Bob Wiggins's excellent text is now in its third edition is testimony to its value for organizations of all kinds. The management of information generally and the control of organizational documentation in particular has been faced by new technological challenges in the decade since the previous edition. The author manages to ride the waves of all the changes that have taken place and brings a calm and considered approach to management problems. This is a book not only for the professional information manager, but also for the general manager who needs a guide through the potential jungle of document management.' (Tom Wilson, Professor Emeritus, University of Sheffield, UK)

'This book made me laugh; not many information management books have achieved that! The laughter was because it correctly states what to many should be obvious when often, sadly, even for records/information managers, it is not. The format and topic based structure makes reading easy on the eye and the brain and facilitates knowledge capture by any reader, not just the information specialists. The Introduction gives a straightforward canter through history, reminding us of many information mediums, and the restructuring is timely, bringing in 'data management as a topic in its own right'. The content is aimed at a wide variety of users, from business managers to information end users. It is an essential read for both new and experienced information managers for its advances in learning and its reference value.' (Paul Dodgson, professional Records and Information Manager and past Vice-Chairman of the Information and Records Management Society)

Readers may contact the author at curabyte@gmail.com.

www.ingramcontent.com/pod-product-compliance
Lightning Source LLC
Chambersburg PA
CBHW051027180526
45172CB00002B/492